90 Reflections From God, From Iowa, From Me

90 Reflections From God, From Iowa, From Me

Ashley Buchanan

XULON PRESS

Xulon Press
2301 Lucien Way #415
Maitland, FL 32751
407.339.4217
www.xulonpress.com

Paperback ISBN-13: 978-1-6628-5706-5
Ebook ISBN-13: 978-1-6628-5707-2

This book is dedicated to:

My Grandmother Mary & My Mother Regina

The two of you are the most influential women in my life. I remember wanting to be just like the both of you! As a little girl, there was nobody else I wanted to please more or whose opinions mattered more. Thank you for shaping me into the person I am today. I hope I can continue to make you both proud.

Mom, as your firstborn we have been together the longest and taught each other the most. Thanks for putting up with me for so long and for being my rock. I'm glad you're not just my mom but also my friend!

Grandma G, I hope that when you're looking down on me from Heaven that you can smile and approve of how my life continues to unfold as I chase my dreams. Thank you for always believing in me! Keep looking out for me because I can be a bit of a mess sometimes! I look forward to the day when I can see you again! I love you the most! All my love xoxoxoxoxo

Special thanks to:

The staff at Xulon Press for all of your hard work. Becoming a published author has been a lifelong dream of mine and I genuinely appreciate you helping me to make this dream a reality!

Mrs. Darlene Turner,

I've never forgotten that fateful day that God allowed our paths to cross. I was stuck between wanting to publish a book and how to get it done. God knew I needed some guidance and with your advice you sent me in the right direction. The world needs more people like you who are willing to help others by your example. You could have easily brushed me off but you didn't. I'll never forget your kindness. I hope God allows our paths to cross several more times. I would love the opportunity to get to know you better!

My Aunt Kendra,

I have always thought of you as the "glue" in our family. You have always been there and helped hold the family together through difficult times. Nobody else can do what you've done over the years as selflessly or efficiently. I know you have sacrificed a lot because you have an enormous heart for God and others. I don't know where I would be today without you and your prayers over my life. I'm truly blessed to have you in my life. I love you!

Brenda and Corinne, (my buddies)

Thank you for all your help letting me use your computer, helping me send emails to my publisher, and the nights we've had supper together hanging out and watching Stranger Things! I love you guys!

Foreword

Writing is one of the few things that come naturally to me. My whole life I have always wanted to be a published author. Many different pieces of this puzzle of my first book have slowly fallen into place throughout the last several years. God has led me from being a young teenager with no direction for my life who didn't even always believe in God, to a slightly older Christian woman who has learned quite a bit about what it is like to have a relationship and spiritual journey with our Creator.

Christianity can be hard to grasp for new converts. I struggled hard for many years. I had a lot to learn on my own. I had to overcome a lot of obstacles. Some of which included fear, doubt, lack of self worth, confusion, and patience. Not only that but I like to think that just by living and experiencing things as I grew older also taught me quite a bit. My goal with this book is to help new converts understand Christianity much quicker and easier than I did. What better way than sharing some of my experiences so that I can relate with someone on a more personal level? You will probably find some common themes throughout these devotionals. I love to write what I'm most passionate about and what I know most. Some of these include the love of God, learning to love and accept ourselves, forgiving ourselves because none of us are perfect, chasing your dreams/success, setting goals, and never giving up.

It took me a while to get serious about writing and even then it took me a while to stick with it. In the end I knew it had to be done because I knew God wasn't going to let me have any peace if I didn't. Countless days or weekends would pass and I would hear the still small voice of God reminding me that I needed to write. The voice wasn't so small after long periods of time trying to drown it out and ignore it. It is only too easy to let life and all its challenges wear us out and get in the way of what God wants us to accomplish with our lives. If we're not careful we can get so caught up with everything else that we just lose track of time all together. Months and years can fly by and leave us wondering how it happened! I fell into that trap often.

I chose to write a devotional because God kept bombarding my mind with so many different thoughts. I could hear a lot of them playing on repeat and crowding each other as if they were fighting to get out. The only way for me to get any sort of relief was to get them out of my head and onto paper. So, in a way, writing is therapeutic to me as much as my now published book will hopefully be an encouragement to somebody else. These are not all my thoughts. I'm no spiritual guru! I believe all my thoughts that I penned down are inspired by God. I just listened to Him.

I also believe we are meant to help others. If some of the things I faced and overcame can help someone else, th0en great, because that means I didn't face these things for no reason and the things that I learned along the way didn't go to waste. Since I can't physically sit down and have a conversation about God with fellow Christians and new converts, I believe a book is the next best option. This book, in many ways is like a projection of my beliefs and my heart. So another goal of mine with this book is to send it out into the world where people can bring it home to read at their leisure. I hope that when you read this that it will feel like I'm sitting next to you having a discussion with you. I don't think I'm the next genius by any means, so I don't want to come across as if I'm lecturing anybody or as if you have to adopt what I believe. I just want to share my experiences and point others in God's direction!

Your Friend,
Ashley Buchanan

DAY 1

Exodus 19:5

*N*ow therefore, if ye will obey my voice indeed, and keep my covenant, then ye shall be a peculiar treasure unto me above all people: for all the earth is mine

I've always been a supporter of having a life verse. At one point I remember searching the Bible for one and I had read the whole Bible and didn't find one that spoke to me. I was a little disappointed but I figured I may as well try it again and the second time around it was this verse that spoke to me. I know different verses help at different stages in your life. For me it has always been this verse that has given me so much encouragement and hope throughout the years. Whenever I'm feeling down, or life hits me pretty hard and I feel like giving up, just reading this verse always helps me dust myself off, take a deep breath and keep going. I encourage you to find a verse that God can use to speak to you when times get tough.

I always try to stay in tune with God. Whenever He gives me an idea, I try my best to allow Him to reveal to me what He would have me share. Some could argue that these ideas are mine and they would be partly correct. Yes, I wrote them but without God I couldn't write anything. God is the one who gifted me the ability to write and a creative mind. He also put an intense desire in my heart to share the truths hidden in the Bible with other believers as He specifically reveals certain things to me through writing. It was during one of these times as I was sitting

1

and meditating on this verse in particular that He revealed some new, mind blowing, and exciting evidence that I had never seen before. God broke this verse down into three parts:

1) God gave us a proposition
   Now therefore, if ye will obey my voice indeed, and keep my covenant
   He gave us a guideline of what He expects us to do. The keyword though is IF. He won't force us and He knows we can choose not to do these two things. However,

2) God attached a promise to His proposition
   Then ye shall be a peculiar treasure unto me above all people: God loves everybody equally. He is not contradicting Himself by saying we could be a peculiar treasure to Him above all others. For one reason His proposition is extended to everybody. Another reason is simply this: when has God blessed someone who is openly, blatantly living in sin? Now consider the word treasure. When I think about treasure, I think about something valuable that I want to guard and keep safe. By choosing to follow God's proposition He is promising to hold us in a higher regard than those who do not.

3) God makes a point
   For all the earth is mine.
   How mind blowing is it that God owns the world and all the people in it, but He wants to single us out by protecting us, setting us apart from everyone else and lifting us up above the rest!

I hope this has helped you understand and appreciate this verse like I do and that it can help you like it has helped me!

3 Wishes

*A*s a kid I loved the Disney movie Aladdin. I was inspired by the idea of finding a magic lamp with a genie inside who would be able to grant me any three wishes. With the exceptions:

1) He can't kill anybody
2) He can't make someone fall in love with you
3) He can't bring anybody back from the dead
4) (This rule is implied) No wishing for more wishes

I couldn't tell you how many times I would daydream about what my three wishes would be. Now that I'm older and am a Christian, I'm glad I don't have to rely on chance of coming across a genie who is only limited to granting me three wishes. I have a heavenly father who loves me enough to provide all my needs in addition to whatever I ask.

Psalm 37:4
Delight thyself also in the Lord;
and he shall give thee the desires of thine heart

Matthew 21:22
And all things, whatsoever ye shall ask in prayer, believing, ye shall receive

I know God does not exist to serve me and answer my prayers out of duty or obligation like a genie. That's not the point. The point is that God serves us and answers our prayers out of love for us. God loves to come through for his children. When we serve him and obey him, he loves to bless us. Perhaps, we ought not to serve God through a sense of duty or obligation like many of us are guilty of doing, or have done in the past. I wonder what would happen if we all started serving God out of our love for him. Maybe that would unlock the door for more blessings and that in abundance. God is not limited to answering three prayers as a genie is to granting wishes.

Philippians 4:19
But my God shall supply all your need according to his riches in glory by Christ Jesus.

We are not limited to the amount of prayers we have. As long as our prayers remain unlimited, the answers to our prayers are unlimited.

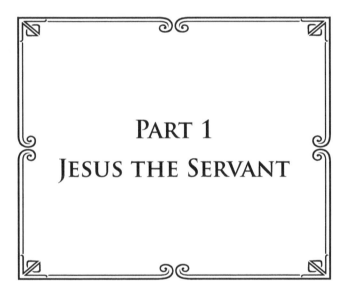

Part 1

Jesus the Servant

Jesus' Purpose For His Life

Mark 10:45

*For even the son of man came not to be ministered unto, but to minister,
and to give his life a ransom for many*

In about two sentences Jesus just revealed his purpose for his life.

1) To minister (or serve) others
2) To give his life a ransom for many (to save)

The emphasis for today being on Jesus' purpose as a servant. You can read for yourself all the miracles Jesus performed. He has a servant's heart! If somebody was blind, he helped them see. If somebody couldn't walk, he healed their legs. Jesus fed people when they were hungry. He even raised people from the dead because He was asked to! If that isn't serving, I don't know what is.

In John 13 you can read where Jesus washes the disciples' feet. Today, that might seem kind of strange, but back then it was a really nice gesture. Sort of like filling up someone's car with gas or buying them dinner in today's world. In Jesus' day, people walked everywhere so their feet would become dusty and dirty from their sandals. Not only was Jesus serving His disciples that day, He was trying to teach them something important. I love Peter's reaction to Jesus washing his feet because I imagine I probably would have reacted the same way. Peter tells Jesus, "You will never wash my feet." I'm sure Peter didn't mean to sound rebellious, but he probably felt as if he wasn't worthy to have the son of God serve him but that he should be serving Jesus by washing his feet instead! Jesus responds by saying, "If I don't wash your feet, you have no part with me." I can imagine Peter now as he says, "In that case, don't just wash my feet but my hands and my head also!" For some reason I picture Jesus laughing and I laugh at that too because I relate to Peter sometimes because I feel like I need a good washing too from all my sins. Jesus tells Peter, "Just having your feet washed this time is good enough."

All we need is to be washed by Jesus' blood once and it is good enough for all the sins we've already committed and for all the sins we haven't committed yet.

DAY 4

Let's Do Some Math!

Genesis 22:17
*That in blessing I will bless thee, and in multiplying I will multiply thy
seed as the stars of heaven, and as the sand which is upon the seashore;
and thy seed shall possess the gate of his enemies.*

If you're anything like me, math doesn't excite you! I've never
been particularly good at that subject growing up or even
now. However, this verse talks about some math that even
I can understand and get excited about. This might seem pretty basic
but bear with me! With that being said, in order to obtain more of
something that would mean it was added to you. That is generally a
good thing! Multiplication is a form of addition. It would be like having
something added to you in larger quantities at once. That is what God
wants to do in our lives. He is always giving and when He gives it is
always in the form of multiplication.

On the other hand, we know that Satan is the opposite of whatever
God is or does the opposite of whatever God does. If God builds, Satan
destroys. If God blesses you by multiplication, (adding to you in large
quantities at once) then it is safe to assume Satan will do the opposite.
He will try to destroy you by using division. Division is a form of sub-
traction because he is taking away from you. Except, Satan desires to
take away from you in large quantities at once.

The reason why is simple. Satan hates you and me so he tries to destroy us. God loves us and He wants to bless us. God wants to build us up and see that we prosper. Nobody can count all the stars or the grains of sand. God has made it clear that He wants to bless us to this magnitude. Honestly, we already are in a lot of ways, but that doesn't mean God is finished with any of us yet! He still has more work to do in and for us. I'm excited to see what God has in store for my life and I hope you can be excited about what God is doing in your life too. Maybe even a victory in some area is coming your way. God did say we shall possess the gate of our enemies!

Casting Your Pearls Before Swine

Matthew 7:6
*Give not that which is holy unto the dogs, neither cast
ye your pearls before swine, lest they trample them under their feet,
and turn again and rend you.*

This verse is so rich! I absolutely love it because it has helped me a lot recently and I hope it will help you too. Imagine taking a string of pearls and dropping them into a pig pen. Hopefully nobody would actually do that because that would literally be insane! I'm sure you would agree. The pigs in that pig pen would not understand or appreciate the value of that pearl necklace. They would trample on it, cover it in mud and their own waste, or even try eating it! The pigs are not worthy of your valuable jewelry and if you threw your jewelry in the pig pen it would be a waste.

Have you ever thought about the possibility of comparing some people in your life to pigs? Maybe it's that relative who always comes to you for money because they know you will give it to them but they don't truly appreciate your sacrifice. Maybe it's a co-worker who always asks for your advice but never takes it and applies it. STOP wasting good things on people who don't appreciate them! There has to come a point in time when you realize that person(s) is not worthy of what you have to offer. This is true for relationships too! If your significant other that you're dating doesn't appreciate you and recognize your value, then they don't deserve you! They don't deserve your time, talents, abilities, affection, money, etc. Please recognize your worth and don't waste yourself on anyone anymore. This might come across as harsh but maybe this will help you see areas in your life where people, (pigs) are actually trampling all over you. YOU are the string of pearls! You need to recognize your worth! You are very valuable!

Lastly, look at the end of this verse. To rend means to tear or rip apart. Pigs already can't see or comprehend value. Once your usefulness to them runs out, they will turn on you and hurt you. Emotionally speaking, there could be a pig in your life who could end up causing you great heartache. Most of us can't always see this at first. I couldn't. Now that I do, I hope you can too!

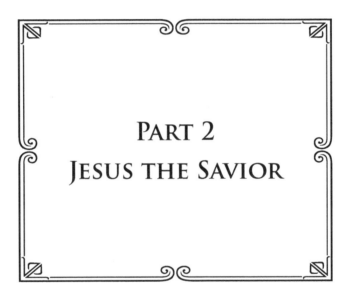

PART 2
JESUS THE SAVIOR

Jesus' Purpose for His Life

Mark 10: 45
For even the son of man came not to be ministered unto,
but to minister, and to give his life a ransom for many.

oday's focus is on the second half of the verse. Some of you who are reading this might think of a ransom in terms of maybe somebody kidnapping a child from a wealthy family. The abductor places a price on the child's head. If the parents pay that price, the child would be returned safely. Much like this scenario, we too were bought back with a price. Before the fall of man we should have been born already belonging to the family of God. However, since the fall of man, we were cursed to enter into the world as sinners by birth. We don't automatically belong to God, we belong to the enemy. Jesus paid our ransom when he died on the cross. Every person alive today or is yet to be born can be covered by Jesus' blood and returned to God's family. Their rightful family. Sadly, most people live their whole lives never realizing this. Some even reject the opportunity to belong to the family of God because they reject Jesus. Everybody's situation is different so it's uneasy to assume why people reject salvation. It could be pride, maybe they believe the lies from the enemy and think they have time later, or maybe they believe they can earn their way to Heaven. Whichever the case may be, I can promise you that there is no reason worth dying and spending eternity separated from God in Hell. Hell is just as real as Heaven and was never meant for anyone else except the devil. Satan just hates God and is trying to destroy everything God has created. Including you and me. So his goal is to take as many people to Hell with him that he can. Of course he would tell you not to worry about it now, or maybe he would convince you that there's nothing to worry about. He'll tell you whatever he needs to in order for you to believe him and stay under his control! Even whom you and I would consider "good people" will still go to Hell if they have not received Christ as savior.

1 Corinthians 6:20
For ye are bought with a price:
therefore glorify God in your body, and in your spirit, which are God's.

You may have heard that salvation is a gift. It is! It doesn't cost us anything because Jesus bought it and paid the price for our ransom. If you choose to reject it then sooner or later you will have to pay. In this case the ransom is not an amount of money or any material thing. The ransom is your soul and it will cost you an eternity of suffering. Friend, don't let that be you. It's time to stop listening to the lies of the enemy and come back to your rightful family!

DAY 7

Don't Look Back

Luke 9:62
*And Jesus said unto him, No man, having put his hand to the plough,
and looking back, is fit for the kingdom of God.*

With many things in life you are required to look forward. When you walk, drive, fly in a plane etc. It wouldn't make sense to do these things backwards. In this example from scripture a farmer ploughs his field forward and has no need to ever look back. If he loses focus and looks backward he might mess up the work he's trying to accomplish. I think it's the same with our calling in life. Spiritually, when God puts us to the plough and we decide to commit to doing His work, we shouldn't look back either. Meaning we should never desire for our lives to return to the state they were when Christ was absent from our lives. Sure, the more you learn the truth the more accountable and responsible you become. That can be scary. Maybe life seemed simpler stuck in your own little bubble when you didn't have many concerns.

For me though, my worst day as a Christian is better than my best day as an unbeliever. For 16 years I faced hurt and hardships alone. I struggled to find peace and any sense of self worth. I always felt like I didn't belong anywhere and that my life had no purpose. I listened to the lies that told me I would never amount to anything and that I would be better off dead. I had no hope for my future. I was just living one day at a time. I was just alive because my heart continued to beat, my lungs kept drawing breath, and my eyes woke up each day. Otherwise I was completely empty inside. My walls I built around myself got a little bit taller, my circle of trust got a little bit smaller.

Now, for about 12 years I've faced a lot more with Jesus by my side. I wouldn't trade that for anything. Even on days when I want to give up I can feel His peace and strength pick me back up. Even if it's slow, He does help me to continue on in spite of my weaknesses. Now I know where all the lies come from. God helps me to recognize them and shoot them down. I know I can never be harmed or defeated. I know I am loved and wanted. I also know I have a very important role to play with my life. I wouldn't trade knowing any of this, nor would I trade knowing where my soul would spend eternity when I die. I didn't know this before and it used to bother me. As far as I'm concerned, there's nothing to go back to.

In Genesis 19 you can read about Lot and his family. God had decided to destroy the cities of Sodom and Gomorrah because of their wickedness. So God warned Lot and his family to leave. Once they did, God sent fire and brimstone to burn up the two cities and all the inhabitants. However, God also instructed them not to look back as they fled their home. Why? Because, they would be leaving everything behind and might be tempted to turn back. Lot's wife had trouble with this instruction. She turned to look back at her home she was leaving behind. Perhaps in anguish and despair in having to leave. Maybe she was already regretting her decision to leave. As a result, she was immediately reduced to a pillar of salt. God allowed her to be burned up along with everything else. I believe in her heart, she turned her back on God and paid the price for it. Notice how her name wasn't even worth mentioning. As far as we know, her name was Lot's wife. God desired for them to be saved from the peril that was sure to follow. He wanted the best for them. What is God telling you? Where is He trying to lead you? Will you trust Him if it means leaving behind your current circumstances?

Almost Only Counts in Horseshoes and Hand Grenades

You are probably familiar with the saying," Almost only counts in horseshoes and hand grenades." The saying is pretty self explanatory considering in a lot of circumstances, almost just isn't good enough. Either you win or you lose. You make a good decision or a bad one. You can say "I almost won!" But it still wouldn't change the fact that you lost.

In the Bible, I'm reminded of an "almost" situation. In Acts you can read about a man named Paul who was once referred to as Saul. Saul persecuted Christians because of their faith in Christ. Eventually, he is converted to Christianity and begins to spread the news of his conversion. Shortly before Paul returns to Jerusalem to witness to the people there, he is warned on more than one occasion not to go. I believe he felt called to go anyway, which he did. To make a long story short, the Jews were offended by what he said and they have him arrested. In Acts 23:11 God appears to Paul and tells him he must witness in Rome just as he did in Jerusalem.

It is in Rome where Paul is sent to be judged before King Agrippa. Paul tells the same story of his life before conversion, how he was converted, and how he now travels spreading the truth. Finally, Paul asks King Agrippa "Do you believe what the prophets say?" King Agrippa responds," Almost thou persuadest me to be a Christian."

Paul presented his case very well. He did what God wanted him to do by witnessing to the king and to the others who were present, but it was still not good enough to convert the king. At this point it's out of Paul's control. The king made a foolish decision that day to reject Christ. Who knows why he did? One could only speculate. Maybe he lived a life of comfort and was afraid it would be ruined. Maybe he was concerned what others around him would think. It could even have been that he thought that he would have another opportunity later in life to accept Christ.

Personally, I didn't want to take that chance. The first time someone explained to me my need for Christ, I jumped at the opportunity. I have never regretted it since. On the other hand I believe King Agrippa has and will continue to regret his decision for the rest of eternity.

DAY 9

The Importance of a Mentor

Proverbs 1:5
A wise man will hear, and will increase learning;
and a man of understanding shall attain unto wise counsels:

Proverbs 11:14
Where no counsel is, the people fall:
but in the multitude of counselors there is safety

*I*n the Bible, a woman named Hannah is recorded to have been sorely grieved by the fact that she had no children. Her husband's other wife had given him children and would mock Hannah for being unable to do the same. Hannah became so grieved that she wept and refused to eat. She reached out to the Lord and prayed to him for a son promising that she would dedicate him to the Lord for the rest of her son's life. God heard her prayer and blessed her with a son which she named Samuel.

Once Samuel was old enough to survive without her, Hannah kept her promise to God and gave her son to the priest Eli. Under Eli's guidance, Samuel was prepared for great and mighty things. Samuel even took over for Eli once he died because Eli's own sons were found to be unfit. The Bible records Eli's sons as being wayward and leading sinful lives.

Fortunately, the majority of us are not separated from our families at young ages like Samuel in order to be used by God. Today, God puts other mentors in our lives. Parents, teachers, preachers and friends could all be mentors because they have your best interests in mind. As long as these individuals give you sound advice based off the teachings from the Bible, then it is ok to take their advice. These leaders recognize the need for everyone to have someone in their lives that can help keep them accountable.

Accountability is almost a foreign concept these days. As a new Christian, I hated hearing that word because I didn't understand it. I thought it was all about control. I thought my authority figures at the time just wanted to know "everything about my life" so they could control me. Now, I've come to think of accountability differently. Accountability helps me stay on target with my goals and dreams. I often tell some of my closest friends about things I plan on doing that way I won't be tempted to back out later. Sometimes just thinking about some of my friends who have similar standards as me, helps me to not get off track because I know they are counting on me. I'm blessed to have several friends I can go to for advice. They have helped me make the best decisions possible that have saved me a lot of stress and heartache. They haven't always been easy or perfect decisions because that isn't real life. However, I do know my life would look very different without those key individuals helping to guide me through those tough times. I encourage everyone to find someone to help hold you accountable and who can give you godly advice concerning your wellbeing and future.

Day 10

P.M.A

Philippians 4:8

Finally, brethren, whatsoever things are true, whatsoever things are honest, whatsoever things are just, whatsoever things are pure, whatsoever things are lovely, whatsoever things are of good report: if there be any virtue, and if there be any praise, think on these things.

A handful of years ago I was given some opportunities to associate with really ambitious, successful, goal oriented people. Among one of the many things I learned from them is the importance of a positive mental attitude. In addition to what it was and the importance of it, I also learned how to apply it. Now, before I go any further, hear me out. I was at first skeptical too. I would meet all these new people who seemed so happy it was almost sort of weird. I would think to myself, "There's no way they are really this happy. There's something wrong with them." So, as critical and negative as I was I actually thought there was something wrong with them for being too happy! I certainly didn't wake up one day and suddenly have all these positive thoughts and was totally happy. Neither did these people. They chose to align their lives according to the above mentioned verse, and when I started to do the same thing, my life improved drastically. Yours can too!

Applying a positive mental attitude is difficult because it takes commitment. As humans we have natural tendencies to be negative. If you have ever put yourself down, complained, worried about finances, etc those are all negative. What I had to learn first was to put a stop to all my negative thoughts. I even practiced cutting off negative thoughts before they were finished and following them up with a positive thought. Eventually, I even began feeling better about myself. Then, circumstances beyond my control didn't bother me as much. Before long I found myself speaking more positively. Our words all begin as thoughts whether we realize it or not. So if you speak negatively, it's because you're thinking negatively.

I truly believe God places a high value on our thoughts because He recognizes the importance of our thoughts. Every thought does matter. Contrary to false beliefs you can control your mind and filter out the negative thoughts. 2 Corinthians 10:5 admonishes us to bring into captivity every thought to the obedience of Christ. You can control your mind. Your mind doesn't have to control you. You hold the power to think the way you choose to. I want to challenge you to do what I have done and cut out the negative from your mind. The next time you feel discouraged remember the verse Romans 8:37 Nay, in all these things we are more than conquerors through him that loved us.

DAY 11

Cast Your Stone

Romans 3:23
For all have sinned, and come short of the glory of God;

very single person who has ever lived has sinned. It is in our nature and not one of us could ever live our entire life without sinning. There will be consequences and judgment for our sins but, I'm a firm believer in letting God do the judging. I also believe that God judges what hasn't been forgiven. When God forgives, He forgets, therefore, how can He judge you for something He forgot about? I'm so thankful that no matter what I do God is always willing and able to forgive me. With that being said, I've learned not to be so judgmental of others.

If you read John 8:1-11 you'll read about a woman caught in the act of adultery. There were people with stones in their hands ready to throw at this woman and persecute her to death. They asked Jesus what he thought they should do and Jesus answered, "He that is without sin among you, let him first cast a stone at her." Every single person was convicted because they were reminded of their own sins. Eventually, everyone dropped their stones and left, leaving only Jesus and the woman who had been accused. The story ends with Jesus forgiving the woman.

A lot of times I'm reminded by this illustration when I want to judge somebody. I ask myself, "What right do I have to throw this stone at them?" So, I do my best to forget about the issue and move on with my life. We need to let go of some issues and leave them to God to deal with. Do you think if someone did you wrong, God is actually going to let them get away with it? Absolutely not!

I hope this helps the next time you want to judge someone, or even if you feel like you're being judged. Wouldn't you want the others to reconsider their decision to attack you? Maybe not physically, but in today's world, verbally. People today are quick to judge by spreading gossip with their tongues. Evaluate yourself and your own mistakes before throwing that stone. Go ahead and lay it down, walk away and forget about the situation. Move on with your life and spend your time and energy on a worthier cause to fight for.

DAY 12

Even the Devil Needs Permission

Job 1:12
*And the Lord said unto Satan, Behold, all that he hath
is in thy power; only upon himself put not forth thine hand.
So Satan went forth from the presence of the Lord.*

*I*n this chapter God is bragging about Job to Satan. Satan basically says, "Well, you're protecting him and blessed him a lot. Anybody would be faithful to you for that. If you take it all away he will turn his back on you." So, God gave Satan permission to take away all of Job's blessings. Most of us know how that story goes. Job lost everything including all his children. Eventually, Job's health is afflicted, his wife turns on him and even his friends are not any comfort. They give him bad advice suggesting he did something to deserve the wrath of God. Through all the trials, Job never once turned his back on God. As a result, God blessed Job with twice as much as he had before.

God knew the outcome the entire time. He had a plan. Job has always been an inspiration to me because as bad as things seem to get sometimes, they've never been as bad as what Job went through. If he could stay faithful through all of that, I could stay faithful through whatever I may face. It also helps me to know that whatever comes my way only does so because God permits it.

1 Corinthians 10:13

There hath no temptation taken you but such as is common to man: but God is faithful, who will not suffer you to be tempted above that ye are able; but will with the temptation also make a way to escape, that ye may be able to bear it.

God knows exactly what we can handle. He allowed Job to go through a pretty tough test and maybe you feel like you are too. Just know that the harder the test, the more you are learning, growing and capable of handling. Whatever you're going through, somebody else couldn't handle. You're stronger than you think you are. It has been said, "The size of the problem is determined by the size of the person." If you have a big problem, you are a bigger person. No matter what comes, do not give up hope. Trust God to take care of you through the whole process and your result will be blessings beyond your imagination.

Day 13

SALT

Matthew 5:13
*Ye are the salt of the earth: but if the salt have lost his savor,
wherewith shall it be salted? It is thenceforth good for nothing,
but to be cast out, and to be trodden under foot of men.*

There are numerous uses for salt. Among them being to add flavor to food, preserve food, clean, and thaw snow and ice. Salt is definitely a good thing. However, if you have too much salt, it could also be bad. The same salt that is useful in melting snow or ice on the roads can rust your vehicles. If you take in too much salt in your body it can dehydrate you and cause a number of health issues. Even while adding flavor to food, too much salt can leave you with a bitter taste.

I think by comparing us to salt, Jesus wants us to be perfectly balanced like the perfect amount of salt. Sure, we're supposed to be different from everyone else because we're Christians. We're supposed to lead others to Christ by our examples. Just not in the sense of being too extreme because then you end up coming off too strong and could end up pushing people away from Christ.

An example of this in my life comes from when I was around 11 years old. For a period of time my sister and I had a babysitter who was a Christian. She let us know all about it! Instead of letting me come to her in my own time she tried forcing her beliefs on me. She would tell me things I should or shouldn't do, or tell me what I should or shouldn't like. I didn't like the idea of her coming into our home and trying to control me and change my life. As a result, she ended up pushing me away from God. I remember thinking to myself how this woman was crazy and if all Christians are like this then I didn't want to be one. I figured I was just fine with how my life was without all her crazy ideas and restrictions that didn't make sense to me. I preferred her to just leave me alone and keep her opinions about God to herself.

Had her approach been different maybe I wouldn't have been turned off from the gospel. Looking back I can see where her actions caused a lot of damage and sowed bad seeds into my mind. For several years I was completely turned off by anything to do with God because of that and she had only been in my life for a brief period of time. Nobody wants the gospel shoved down their throats. Take time to get to know the people you want to witness to. Find out what is important to them and go from there. Start building a relationship and establish some trust with that individual so that they will be more receptive to what you have to say. Ultimately, God will need to do a majority of the work anyway but we make it way more difficult than it should be when we leave a bad taste with people and rub them the wrong way.

PART 1

THE LIGHT:
GOD IS LIGHT

DAY 14

The Light: God Is Light

Psalm 27:1 a
The Lord is my light and my salvation; whom shall I fear?

John 1:1
*In the beginning was the Word, and the Word was with God,
and the Word was God*

Psalm 119:105
Thy word is a lamp unto my feet, and a light unto my path.

he concept that God is light has brought me so much inspiration! I can only hope to scratch the surface of understanding it. For starters let's establish the fact that the Bible (also known as the Word of God) IS God! He wrote it, it came from Him. It is a gift of himself that He gave to us to read, and hold in our hearts and minds. When we hold our Bibles we are holding God. When we read them, we are reading God's thoughts, promises and predictions. If you want the knowledge of God and want to know how He thinks, read the Bible.

Next, lamps are tools that produce light. They are very useful because without them, we wouldn't be able to see in the dark. We would stumble all over the place, run into things, possibly jam your toe into something....very painful! If God is His word, and His word is light, Psalm 119:105 could be paraphrased as God is a lamp unto my feet and a light unto my path. Wherever God is, there is light. If you take God away from the equation, there will be darkness. God doesn't need a lamp like we do because He is a living lamp. If you have spiritual darkness in your life, reading the Bible will illuminate the way you should go. It will reveal answers to your problems. Likewise, if you take the Bible out of your life, don't read it or apply it, you will have spiritual darkness in your life. Through reading and applying what we learn from the Bible, we are utilizing God's light to detect things in our life that are harmful to us so we can avoid them. Otherwise, without it, how will you be able to avoid trouble, hurt and pain in the dark? Not only that, but if you were charting unfamiliar territory in the dark, doesn't it give you a sense of unease or fear because you can't see what might be lurking nearby? With God illuminating your life you will be able to avoid trouble, pain and eliminate any fear.

PART 2

THE LIGHT:
WE ARE LIGHT

The Light: We Are Light

1 Peter 2:21
For even hereunto were ye called: because Christ also suffered for us, leaving us an example, that ye should follow his steps:

Matthew 5:14 & 16
Ye are the light of the world: A city that is set on a hill cannot be hid

Let your light so shine before men, that they may see your good works, and glorify your Father which is in heaven

*P*reviously, we established that God is light. Next, I want to show you how we can be light too. Thanks to 1 Peter 2:21 we already know, throughout the span of our lifetime, we should strive to be like Christ. One of the best ways to accomplish this is by reading His word and memorizing it. Don't misunderstand me. I'm not saying you have to memorize the Bible cover to cover. But you should start somewhere. Start with whichever verses speak to you the most and give you strength. Then you will know when the enemy is feeding you a lie. By memorizing scripture, you will literally have God abiding or living in you! Do you understand, once you begin to do this, by default you become light! That's why in Matthew chapter 5, God compares us to light because we are like God! Light exists because of God. We exist because of God. When you think about it, darkness doesn't really exist. Darkness is just a result from an absence of light. Darkness has no substance. It serves no purpose. It can't give life like the light does. It is common knowledge that plants need sunlight to grow. There have been studies that confirm people who live in colder, rainier regions where the sun doesn't shine as often, are more likely to experience depression.

With that being said, God compels us to shine our light. This might be cliché but think of yourself as a lighthouse. You serve a special purpose to those lost in the sea of life. People will be attracted to you. They will look to you for help. It is our responsibility to then point these people in God's direction. After all, He gave us our light and we will only have true shelter and safety by abiding in Him.

DAY 16

Too Much Blood in the Fight

Read John 19: 1-30

You just read about Jesus being scourged, crucified and his death.
I'll never forget a message I once heard explaining in depth Jesus'
crucifixion and exactly how painful it would have been. Scourging,
I learned, was the use of a whip on somebody. Except, this was no
ordinary whip. It was a whip with nine tails, each tail embedded with
sharp pieces of bone. This whip was designed to cause extreme pain by
wrapping itself completely around the individual, hooking into their
flesh and tearing it apart each time it is pulled back. After the scourging,
soldiers jammed a crown of thorns onto Jesus' head and began
punching him in his face. Then, the crucifixion. Nailed to a cross, each
nail strategically placed to cause the most pain, our savior bled to death.

So many people would have tucked tail and run after the scourging. Countless others wouldn't even make it to the scourging. There are so many people who are afraid to fight. They are afraid to fight for what's right and what they believe in. They don't have the courage to take a hit. Jesus knew there was too much at stake to quit and give in. He literally had too much blood in the fight. Your life and mine hung in the balance. To take it a step further, everybody's life was at stake. Jesus knew we would depend on him following through and dying to save us. He was our only hope.

Anybody else agree that the best boxing matches to watch are the ones where the underdog finally gains the advantage and miraculously beats the guy who was winning two seconds ago? I can see it now. The underdog just keeps taking hits. Bam! One to the jaw. He is knocked off his feet by the force of the blow. He staggers to his feet, wipes some blood off his lip. Wham! Another punch. This time to his eye. Again, he gets knocked down. Again, he finds the strength to stand back up as blood from the cut in his eyebrow trickles into his eye. He squints, trying to keep his opponent in sight. Every hit he receives strengthens his resolve to get back up one more time! Finally, he finds an opening and gains the advantage. He starts whaling against the other guy. He seized an opportunity and just keeps throwing punches, backing the opponent into a corner. Even then he doesn't stop until he successfully deals the last punch that knocks the guy out cold and he wins.

Personally, in my life when the devil throws punches at me, I try to get back up each time. I wipe off the blood and prepare myself for the next hit. Bam! Car troubles. Pow! Health issues. Wham! No money! Whatever the devil may throw at me, however bleak things look at the time, I remind myself that I'm going to get through this. I know in the end I'm going to win. Romans 8:37 says Nay, in all these things we are more than conquerors through him that loved us. With God on our side we won't lose. The devil will! Every time I get hit, my resolve strengthens. This is too personal. I've got too much blood in the fight to back down now. I just bide my time until I see my opening and I can gain the upper hand. We all, as children of God, have come too far to give up now! Whatever you're going through, God is right there with you. Don't lose heart. Don't be afraid. That's what the devil wants. He wants to get you discouraged. He wants to knock you down and keep you down. Don't give him that satisfaction!

DAY 17

The Devil Belongs Under Your Feet

Genesis 3:15
*And I will put enmity between thee and the woman,
and between thy seed and her seed; it shall bruise thy head,
and thou shalt bruise his heel.*

I have never been a fan of snakes, but even more so when I learned that Satan used a snake to trick Adam and Eve into disobeying God by eating the forbidden fruit. Since then, the serpent has always been symbolic of the devil. After the fall of the human race and everything became cursed, part of the snake's (Satan's) curse was that he would be made as low as possible. So low that he would have to slither around on his belly and no longer have legs to support his body as a means of moving around. Also, because of the serpent's active role in the downfall of humanity, God placed a special hatred between humans and snakes. Snakes are brought so low that while on the ground they shouldn't be able to strike a person very high. Maybe on your leg or your foot, but the bottom line is, we tower over snakes. It might bite us on the leg but we have the ability to stomp on its head and kill it.

Imagine a Chihuahua. I like to refer to them as ankle biters. They can't reach very high to bite you and if they do bite you, it doesn't hurt very much. More than anything, they're just annoying. They're pretty persistent and it's hard to get them to stop attacking you. That's how snakes (Satan) is. He's like a snake that will continuously pester you by attacking your ankles, legs or feet. He's not ever going to stop. We have to stomp on his head. We can't kill him and he can't kill us, but he can and he will continue to attack us. Which is why we must attack him back. More than likely, we will have to stomp on his head a lot throughout the course of our lives. Since he's not going to stop getting in our way and tripping us up, we shouldn't stop stomping on him when he does. The devil got the worst end of the curse. God gave us dominion over all the animals when everything was created and He has never revoked that right. We are rightfully above snakes and Satan. We have power over them, not the other way around. Step confidently into your position of power and remind the devil of where his place is: underneath your feet. Luke 10:19 says Behold, I give unto you power to tread on serpents and scorpions, and over all the power of the enemy: and nothing shall by any means hurt you.

Try as he might, the devil can't actually hurt us. He would like you to believe he can. So, he keeps you trapped by fear, but it's all just an illusion.

DAY 18

1 Peter 5:8
Be sober, be vigilant; because your adversary the devil,
as a roaring lion, walketh about, seeking whom he may devour.

*I*n this verse the devil is compared to a roaring lion. My guess is, if a lion is roaring, he is pretty upset. Angry even. His hunger could be the reason he's angry which would compel him to take action. I believe that is the reason God compares the devil to this kind of lion. The devil is always hungry for destruction. He is always on the move and taking action. The devil, like a hungry lion will do anything for his next meal. He will take risks. He is blinded by his hunger and fueled by his anger. He searches desperately for someone to feast on. He has a purpose and a goal. The devil is desperate, dangerous and destructive.

Ready for the good news? You can kill him! Not literally, but I mean you can kill his attempts at destroying your life. God gave Samson the strength to physically and literally kill a lion with his bare hands by ripping the lion's jaws apart. Here's a little secret for you. God will give you the strength to kill the lions in your life too.

Philippians 4:13
I can do all things through Christ which strengtheneth me.

I'm not the brightest crayon in the box, but I'm pretty sure by "all things," that would include killing a lion, or in this case any of the devil's attempts. God will give me and you the strength to do it. So, yet again, in this scenario the devil comes out as a loser. In the end the devil was always meant to lose and will always lose! This is something I'm actually really glad about because I have this competitive streak in me and I hate losing and love winning! Anybody else relate? Anyway, the main point is, knowing that we're going to win and the devil is going to lose, we should no longer be discouraged when we have to face him. No matter how ferociously he snarls at you, just remember it's all for show because you're staring into the face of a loser. When the devil comes at you and tries to intimidate you by getting in your face, grab his jaws and rip them apart like Samson did with his lion. We are meant to have victory over the devil by thwarting him every time and throwing a wrench in his plans. The devil knows this. That's why he keeps trying to stop us. We're very dangerous to him. Don't let him intimidate you anymore. Maybe he has won against you before but you can change the outcome in the future. Put him back in his place and remind him that he is actually the loser here. Claim your victory!

DAY 19

The Enemy's #1 Strategy

1 Corinthians 1:10
*Now I beseech you, brethren, by the name of our Lord Jesus Christ,
that ye all speak the same thing, and that there be no divisions
among you; but that ye be perfectly joined together in
the same mind and in the same judgement.*

I believe the enemy's number one strategy is to divide and conquer. God wants unity, Satan wants division. We are stronger together than when we are alone. Satan knows this to be true. Think about the climbing divorce rate in America. Think about the number of people who have committed suicide because Satan had them isolated from everyone else, feeding them lies that probably sounded something like this, "Nobody cares about you. You can't trust anyone. You'll never fit in anywhere because you're not good enough. Your life is a waste." It goes on and on. The devil is full of lies. How come when you're working on your relationship with God, the devil throws distractions at you to keep you from praying, reading your Bible or attending church? It's because he's trying to drive a wedge between you and God! You are most definitely a threat to him when you're close to God!

Have you noticed how easy it is to offend somebody these days? A simple miscommunication can send somebody over the edge and they will blow things completely out of proportion. Even something as

45

simple as voicing your opinion about a topic will upset people today. That's nothing but the devil trying to cause strife and division among us. We have to learn to recognize the warning signs to diffuse situations before they occur. If they do happen anyway, we need to make sure we're not "adding fuel to the fire." Don't feed into the devil's attempts to divide.

On the bright side, we can use this same strategy against the devil. We can discover and pinpoint the areas in our life that are being attacked, isolate them by focusing on them and then figure out ways to conquer them. Whatever you're going through, I would pray to God about it, seek counsel from other godly influences, even read books on the subject. I strongly advise to do whatever it takes to resolve the issue because once you conquer it, the next time Satan tries to defeat you by using the same tactic, it will be less effective. I urge you to join or create a group that you can always go to for help and that will always encourage you. That way you will never have to feel isolated because that is when we are the most vulnerable.

DAY 20

There Is Power in Our Words

Luke 1:18
And Zechariah said unto the angel, Whereby shall I know this?
For I am an old man, and my wife well stricken in years.

Words are very powerful. I have heard it said many times that our words hold the power to tear somebody down or to build them up. We need to be careful with what we say. Words are an outward expression of our inward character. To put it another way, our true selves will be displayed through our words. If you are constantly thinking critically about somebody, it will come out in your words. The same is true if you respect someone, you will compliment them or edify them.

God's words have power in them. In case you have forgotten this is true, go back and read the beginning of the Bible how in Genesis it teaches us that God literally spoke the world and everything else into existence. Genesis 1:3 says And God said, Let there be light: and there was light. Everything else that God created, He spoke it and it appeared. I personally believe that God could have chosen for everything to be created just from His thoughts because He is that powerful, but I also think that God wants to teach us about the power our words contain also. You could even read about the life of Jesus. There were many miracles that were performed as a result of his words. Jesus rebuked the storm while he and his disciples were at sea, then the winds and waves calmed down. When Jesus fed four thousand people with seven loaves of bread and a few fish, He first gave thanks to His Father through prayer for what they had and then the miraculous happened. There was enough food for everybody.

I think you're getting the picture. However, if you still doubt the power of our words, and your words, look at the example of Zechariah from today's verse. When an angel appeared to him to tell him his wife was going to have a baby, I believe he first doubted the words of the angel in his heart, because second, he voiced his thoughts to the angel. As a result of his unbelief, the angel took away Zechariah's voice. He spoke out of doubt and during his wife's entire pregnancy he was unable to speak. Only after the birth of their son, John, was Zechariah able to have his voice back. I'm willing to bet Zechariah learned the hard way just how meaningful words actually are and that he was more careful with what he allowed himself to say in the future.

DAY 21

Believing Is Seeing

John 20:29

*Jesus saith unto him, Thomas, because thou hast seen me, thou hast
believed: blessed are they that have not seen, and yet have believed.*

How many times have we said or heard somebody say, "I'll
believe it when I see it." In John chapter 20 that's basically what Thomas is saying. The other disciples have
seen Jesus come back to life after His death and burial and were telling
Thomas about their encounter with Jesus. Thomas didn't believe them
and told them, "I'm not going to believe it until I can see the nail prints
in his hands and feel them or feel his side." Thomas wanted to see and
feel with his own eyes and hands the wounds Jesus received from the
cross in order to believe that He was really risen from the dead. Eight
days after Thomas made that statement Jesus appeared to the disciples
again this time including Thomas. Jesus said to Thomas," Reach over
here and feel my hands. Also, come feel my side, so that you can believe."

Jesus didn't have to prove himself to Thomas, but He did anyway
and I believe that is why He rebuked Thomas for having so little faith.
Because he was one of the disciples, Thomas would have spent a lot of
time with Jesus on a personal level. He would have witnessed firsthand
many of the miracles Jesus performed. Not only that, but Jesus had
told his disciples that He would die and three days later rise from the
dead. I have reason to believe that every single one of them didn't take

Jesus seriously because they were surprised when Jesus actually did. Some of them didn't even recognize Him until He revealed who He was when they did encounter him. Not everybody is fortunate enough to actually meet Jesus while alive on this earth. That is why Jesus says we are blessed because we choose to believe in Him even though we have not ever seen Him. It takes a lot more faith to believe in something or someone that you have never seen. That is why we should walk by faith not by sight. How do you know that the good things you have sown will come up? Faith. How do you know that your prayers will be answered? Faith. How do you know your needs will be met every month? Faith. These are things we can't see either but we must believe anyway.

A Thought About the Rich Young Ruler

Mark 8:36
*For what shall it profit a man,
if he shall gain the whole world, and lose his own soul?*

*I*magine asking someone for advice, they tell you what they think and what you should do and then you decide against it. In other words you throw their advice out the window. Why even bother asking if you are not going to heed their advice? Now imagine that you have just met Jesus and you ask him for his advice in a certain situation. Surely you would follow his advice exactly as he says wouldn't you? For your sake and mine, I should hope we would, but that isn't true for everybody.

Read the scripture Matthew 19:16-24

You just read about a rich young ruler who asked Jesus for advice concerning eternal life. Jesus told him to keep the commandments. The rich young ruler replied," I've kept all those since I was a small child." Jesus then responded," Well, then, sell everything you own and give away your money. Then come and follow me." Jesus' statement was not to point out that salvation was to be obtained by selling his possessions, but rather to reveal to the rich young ruler that he hasn't actually kept the commandments.

If he loved his neighbors as much as he loved himself, he would give to those in need. If he loved Christ, he would follow Jesus. Instead the Bible says in verse 22," the young man went away sorrowful: for he had great possessions."

This might seem harsh but I not only believe this young ruler was materialistic, but I believe he was also selfish. Perhaps he was accustomed to the comfortable lifestyle his wealth provided and that could have been a key factor as to why he didn't want to give it up in order to follow Jesus. After all, even Jesus sometimes didn't have anywhere to lay down his head at night because He was always traveling and serving people. Maybe that was unappealing to the rich young ruler. I do also believe this young man loved his possessions too much to give them up even though his soul hung in the balance. How foolish it seems to let possessions, things, keep someone from salvation. Things are temporary. They fade away and continually get replaced by something bigger or better anyway. The gadgets we have today far exceed anything this young man could have imagined of and it will be the same for us when our descendents walk this earth.

However, by no means does Jesus or myself condemn the rich. There are those who are rich who are Christians. I'm thankful for them and the role they play with their lives that most people can't. In Matthew 19: 23-24 I believe Jesus is describing how difficult it is for those who are already rich to receive salvation because they probably believe they already have everything they need in life. Not that it's impossible, just difficult. Friends, don't be like this young man and place a higher value on things rather than your soul, your God or anyone else in your life for that matter.

Day 23

Confusion

1 Corinthians 14:33
For God is not the author of confusion,
but of peace, as in all churches of the saints.

If God is not the author of confusion, that must mean Satan is. Anything God is, Satan is the opposite. Confusion is real. I think confusion is a result of doubt. If Satan can plant seeds of doubt in your mind then he can cause you to become confused. Almost like the depiction from a cartoon you might be familiar with, where you have an angel on one shoulder and a devil on your other one, each telling you different things. You have God telling you one thing and Satan telling you something completely different. You have to learn to differentiate between the two voices. Otherwise you will be playing right into the hands of the devil. If he can get you to doubt God, then cause you to become confused, most likely what you will do next is nothing! The reason you'll do nothing is because you won't know what's right or wrong and you'll be afraid of doing the wrong thing. You will be frozen by your fear. That's where the devil wins. When he has successfully stopped us from doing whatever it is that God has called us to do. Obviously, the devil wants to stop us because he knows we are a threat to him and his cause.

Contrary to false beliefs, the devil is very smart. He might use some of his same, age old tricks but that's because they still work on us! If more of us could catch on to what is really going on and stop falling for his lies he would be forced to come up with new plans and change things up. He knows enough about right and wrong and even scripture so he can pervert it to make us second guess what we know. Satan is smart enough to know better than to make things too obvious. He creates gray areas and fudges things up just enough that we will compromise on some of our standards or beliefs. We'll begin to settle for less. He is the literal author of confusion. He literally writes it into our minds and publishes it in our hearts. How do you learn to distinguish between God and Satan? Listen to the voice that brings you peace. God is the author of peace. Peace is your sign that you're doing the right thing because even in the midst of your troubles God will be there radiating peace into your soul and mind. I've been in difficult situations where even I had no idea how I could be so calm except for the fact that I knew that God was giving me His peace. The kind of peace that passes all understanding. There's nothing else in the world like it.

DAY 24

What Am I?

Psalm 103: 14
For he knoweth our frame; he remembereth that we are dust.

During some point in your lifetime, you might have heard somebody say," Who am I that God would love me?" This comes from a humble perspective. Yes, we are special, but outside of that, we are not perfect. We don't possess amazing powers such as God has to create things out of nothing but our words. We don't know everything. We are full of sin and make numerous mistakes. Yet, Jesus still chose to die for us.

Life can be confusing. I know I spent years trying to figure out who and what I was. Whenever I reflect on the following questions I am humbled.

1) Who am I that the God of the universe and Creator of everything, would care enough about me to know my name?
2) Why should He think about me?
3) Why should He answer my prayers?
4) Why should He protect me?
5) Why should He have died for me?

The answer to these questions actually doesn't lie in who we are but in who Jesus is. It's in His nature. It's part of His character. It's what makes Him who He is. It's what sets Him apart from us and makes Him worthy of our praise and worship. I honestly can't say that I would do what Jesus did when He died on the cross. Maybe I could see myself dying to protect someone I love and who loves me, but that would be easy to do. Jesus chose to die willingly not only for people He knew loved Him or who would love Him, but also for people He knew who would hate Him, mock Him and reject Him. As far as who I am, I've given it a considerable amount of thought and this is the best I can come up with. Maybe some of you can identify with me. Make this devotional personal to you. Exchange my name and gender with yours.

What: I am a soul. I am bones, tissues, muscles and organs that all function (almost) perfectly together as they should like they were designed to. I am also dust like my ancestors who were formed from the earth when they were created. Dust is what my body will return to when it is old and tired and gives out on me when my purpose on earth is completed and God calls me home to live with Him in Heaven. I am a sinner, but I am also saved.

Who: I am a woman. My name is Ashley Buchanan. I am a child of a king! I am loved by God! I am a Christian. I am somebody who loves God and wants to serve Him for the rest of my life. I am the grand-daughter of Melvin and Mary and George and Edith. I am the daughter of Michael and Regina. I am a big sister. I am a best friend to many people. I am a hard worker and a big dreamer. I am blessed beyond my wildest dreams and have special talents and abilities. I am an author pursuing my calling and my dreams.

DAY 25

Priceless

Proverbs 31: 10
Who can find a virtuous woman? For her price is far above rubies.

Ladies, this devotion is for you! If you are a man reading this, hopefully, it will help you appreciate the women in your life more. (spouse, mother, daughter, sister, niece, etc.) As a woman the world we live in today can be very tough. No matter what stage in life you are at, there is a lot of direct and indirect pressure on us. To name a few: If you're single, you face the difficulties of providing for yourself and meeting your needs alone which can be scary without someone to help you and be there for you when the unexpected hits. You also feel pressure to "find someone" when you see all your friends moving on and your life seems like it's not moving forward at all but standing still. If you're married you feel pressure to be a good wife. If you're a mother, you probably feel pressure to be a good mom, constantly doubting that you're doing a good enough job. Meanwhile we feel pressure to hold down our jobs and take care of the housework. Oftentimes, this causes us to neglect ourselves and our appearances because we're so busy taking care of others and trying to do too much. As a result we can begin to question our worth. Not just in our eyes but in the eyes of those who are important to us as well.

I highly recommend a book called Captivating by John and Staci Eldridge. This book helped me open my eyes to the value of women and

I learned a lot of things about myself that I didn't understand before-hand. In their book, John and Staci call women "the crown of creation." Even the above mentioned verse says your price is far above rubies. There's not a definite price tag on your head because your value is so great, it cannot be priced! Only that it is far above the price of rubies! Far above! Have you ever wondered, as I have many times, why God compares us to rubies? Why not diamonds, emeralds, or pearls? God could have used gold or silver. Personally, gold really attracts my attention. God could have used anything in the world to compare us to, but He chose rubies. Think with me for a moment.... What could possibly be so special about rubies?

Do you give up yet? Rubies are red. Can you think of something else that is red? How about blood? And not just any blood, but the blood of Jesus. The next time you feel insignificant or worthless, just remember that Jesus shed His blood for you. His blood is pure and priceless and that was the price paid for you. Your price is far above rubies! If Jesus believed it to be true and believed you were worth dying for, then it must be true!

DAY 26

Seek Wisdom First

Matthew 6: 33
But seek ye first the kingdom of God, and his righteousness;
and all these things will be added unto you.

In 1 Kings chapter 3 you can read an inspiring passage of scripture about a dream Solomon had where the Lord appeared to him and said," Ask what I shall give thee?" Could you imagine God saying to you," Ask whatever you want from me and I will give it to you."? Solomon could have asked for anything and God would have given it to him. What would you ask for? There have sure been times for me when I would have answered differently than Solomon's request for wisdom. I love the Lord's reaction to Solomon's request. Not only did God honor his request but He also blessed Solomon with everything else he didn't ask for. Solomon was promised longevity of life, victory over his enemies, and immeasurable wealth. It is noted that people from all over the world were attracted to Solomon because of his wisdom and wealth which has surpassed that of any other living person.

I would be willing to bet that Solomon didn't expect God to give him all those blessings. We have the advantage of knowing that God is willing to do the same thing for us thanks to Matthew 6:33. God doesn't promise to give us some of the things we ask for, but He says all these things will be given to us if we seek Him first. What are you needing God to manifest in your life? Is it your health? Do you need God to restore your marriage? Are you struggling to raise your children? Are your finances causing you despair? All these things will be added unto you but you know what you need to do first!

PART 1

YOUR HEART
IS SACRED

DAY 27

Lessons About the Heart

Proverbs 4:23
Keep thy heart with all diligence; for out of it are the issues of life.

The heart is pretty awesome! I'm no expert on how exactly it functions as it sustains our very lives, but I do know it has spiritual functions as well. Our hearts are valuable which is why God wants us to keep them guarded. One reason that makes our hearts valuable is that they contain treasure.

Matthew 6:21
For where your treasure is, there will your heart be also.

Our hearts are basically like a treasure chest. So, what is the treasure? Our thoughts.

Proverbs 23:7
As a man thinketh in his heart so is he.

Our thoughts are valuable because they make us who we truly are. Our words and our actions will reflect the thoughts in our hearts.

Luke 6:45
A good man out of the good treasure of his heart bringeth
forth that which is good; and an evil man out of the
evil treasure of his heart bringeth forth that which is evil:
for of the abundance of the heart his mouth speaketh.

When it comes to guarding our hearts, I like to envision a pirate protecting his treasure. Just as a pirate would fight to protect it or keep it hidden from others, it would be wise for us to do the same with our hearts. Hopefully this will help somebody realize how valuable your heart truly is. Don't just go and give it away to anybody. Not everyone will appreciate its worth. It is a treasure worth keeping close and safe. Maybe that's why it is hidden inside our chest! Your treasure is in your chest!

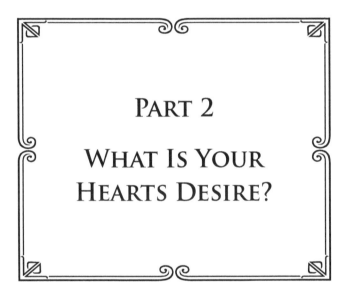

PART 2

WHAT IS YOUR
HEARTS DESIRE?

DAY 28

Lessons About the Heart

Psalm 37:4
Delight thyself also in the Lord;
and he shall give thee the desires of thine heart.

I wasn't always a Christian. Therefore, for a long time, I struggled with believing I was worthy of great things. After I became a Christian and learned about the verse mentioned above, I doubted its validity. For several years I battled myself and really the devil about my self- worth. As I continued growing spiritually, God helped me to identify and accept the truth.

Friend, whatever you're struggling with, you are worthy of bigger and better things in your life! Once I began to accept this new truth about myself, I could more easily evaluate my dreams and desires that were buried deep within my heart. Not only do I believe I can have my desires but I believe I will have them because I've learned how to trust this verse and what God says in general. I know it isn't easy. To some degree faith is essential. To another degree, you just have to believe that God loves you. It is hard to see your own value but when you try and look at yourself through God's eyes you will be able to see that it's true. Accepting yourself and building your self-image will take time, effort and work but it doesn't have to take a long time or be difficult if you rely on God for help.

I encourage you to examine your heart. Discover what desires you have hidden deep in your heart. You are worthy of having your dreams come true and you will have them come true if you start claiming this verse and become bold enough to believe it.

PART 3

BROKEN HEART

Lessons About the Heart

Psalm 147: 3
He healeth the broken in heart, and bindeth up their wounds.

A broken heart can come in many forms. Maybe a family member has let you down. A close friend could have stabbed you in the back. Your child has disappointed you. Someone who you thought would always be in your life has abandoned you. Someone you love has passed away. As you're reading this something has probably come to your mind. In my opinion, a broken heart is unparalleled to any other kind of pain. If something is wrong physically, it is way easier to detect it and to get it treated. When your heart is broken, the best things to help is prayer, time and possibly even crying. I don't know anyone who likes to cry especially not me! Sometimes that is just the only form where we can express ourselves when words won't come and nothing else can be done to help. Sometimes crying is an essential part of healing and there's nothing wrong with that.

At times, the pain from a broken heart can be so overwhelming that you can't pray because you might not even want to at the moment because you can't even process all your thoughts and emotions to form the words to speak. Sometimes you might need to be alone because nobody else can comfort you. Sometimes you might find it hard to get up every day and function as if your life is normal and act like everything is ok when, clearly it isn't. If there's one thing I've learned about healing when you're heartbroken is that everyone heals at different rates. Take all the time you need. Don't let others make you feel bad and don't ever feel like you have to rush yourself.

The next time a relationship ends abruptly and there seems to be no chance of it working out, don't be ashamed if you still feel "stings" a month, or two or three months afterward. It's part of the healing process. I get it. You invested time with that person. You became emotionally attached to them. You had some great times with them. It's hard when you get used to having them actively involved in your life and then they suddenly decide to bail. With prayer and time, you can get past it and you will become a better and stronger person because of it. You can use your pain as an opportunity to learn something from it.

The time will come when you are ready to turn to God for healing. God is the best at healing broken hearts! I hope whatever you are going through, or will go through in the future, that you will give God a chance to heal you. Your recovery will be a lot quicker and smoother!

PART 4

A SICK HEART

DAY 30

Lessons About the Heart

Proverbs 13:12
Hope deferred maketh the heart sick:
but when the desire cometh, it is a tree of life.

UT! I love when God puts a but in a verse because the verse isn't over and it gets better. In the first half of the verse God is simply making a statement. The second half is a promise! I don't know about you, but I love discovering God's promises and claiming them because God always keeps His promises! I also love how this promise is compared to a tree. Trees grow tall and strong. They have multiple branches. Trees are meant to flourish and give life. They give shelter to birds and numerous other animals and insects. Trees also help provide the oxygen we need in order to breathe.

Maybe, right now you feel like your heart is sick because you have been praying for something for a long time. I sometimes feel this way when my payers continue to go unanswered. It's hard to understand and it's hard to continue to be patient. It's even harder to keep praying because we feel like giving up and it seems as if our prayers are not being heard. Look at the word deferred. It means delayed or postponed. It doesn't mean denied. Our requests are not being denied altogether, just delayed until the time is right. Then, when they come, they will be as big and beautiful as a tree! When our prayers become realized, they will branch out into other areas of our lives and affect other people we come in contact with. It will bring life into areas that were previously "dead". You will feel refreshed and others will be able to see the good works God has wrought in you. Just like a tree, you will become strong enough to withstand the storms of life and the bad weather that comes your way. Eventually, others may even come to depend on you for help and shelter when they have nowhere else to go.

We can't give up on our prayers because they will come to fruition and bring fresh life into our lives. It will get better! Just keep hanging on to God's promises. Just like we can't count all the leaves on a tree, we won't be able to count all the ways our life will be blessed when our prayers become answered!

DAY 31

The Dangers of Self Diagnosis

Proverbs 3:7

Be not wise in thine own eyes: fear the Lord, and depart from evil.

This verse can be applied to any area of your life, but I want to share with you an example from my life.

About five years ago my health started failing. I was listening to myself and chose to ignore all the warning signs my body was giving me. I never went to the doctor, and rationalized away all my symptoms. I made up reasons that might explain my odd behavior and blamed stress and lack of sleep etc. on my physical decline. I went on this way for several months only getting worse. By the time some close friends of mine had taken me to the emergency room, if I had waited too much longer, it could have been too late and I wouldn't be here today. At some point in time my pancreas had stopped producing insulin and I was living my life not knowing or even seeking advice as to why I felt so bad all the time. I was living with blood sugar levels of over 500 borderline 600 on a regular basis for several months. Because of the excessive amount of sugar in my blood, my blood had become like a poison in my veins. Every area of my life had been affected by my decline. I was often an emotional wreck, I had withdrawn from some of the most important relationships with friends and family, I had even withdrawn from God. My mind couldn't retain new information for very long, I couldn't walk straight, my vision would get blurry, I was always short tempered and a whole host of other symptoms.

You could say that experience was a major wake up call. Sure, finding out I now had Type 1 Diabetes was definitely not easy because my whole life was turned upside down. As hard as living with this disease is still to this day, yes, part of me wishes it would never have happened. My life could be so much less complicated if I had the power to change things. On the other hand, another part of me (the less selfish part) reminds myself that I have been through other things that were worse and have come out with a positive attitude over those situations, so I can find the positive about my diabetes. The positive being that maybe I'm meant to help somebody else in the future when they get the same diagnosis unexpectedly. I have met an inspirational diabetic counselor who so far has been the only person to break through to me about accepting my diagnosis and learning to move forward with my life. She has been able to connect me to new doctors who care about me as an individual and help me feel motivated to keep making the extra effort to take care of myself when before I didn't feel like it. This diabetic counselor has been able to break through to me the best (mostly because I'm stubborn) but also because she has Type 1 Diabetes and she never beat around the bush, but she also could connect with me on a personal level and not through a cold and professional level. Maybe I am meant to be that inspiration for somebody else.

Also, my relationship with God has been more challenging but even more so rewarding than ever before since my diagnosis. I have a new outlook on life every time I look back on that experience and reflect on all the little ways that God was working behind the scenes to keep me safe. For example all the times I had driven with blurry vision and miraculously made it to my destinations. Even the fact that every day I simply continued to wake up because at any given moment I could have slipped into a diabetic coma and never woken up from it. I am thankful for God protecting me and making it clear to me that He still has plans for me and my life and that is why He chose to keep me on this earth.

Hopefully, some of your experiences, either past or yet to come will not be as drastic as my example. Either way, I hope this will help you and myself in the future to never take our own advice but to take our situation to God and to others. God can use those in our sphere of influence to help us determine what is going on and how we should handle things.

A Fresh Start

2 Corinthians 5:17
Therefore if any man be in Christ, he is a new creature:
old things are passed away; behold all things are become new.

I always like when a new year rolls around because that gives
me a fresh start at bettering myself and getting a new plan
in place that will help me accomplish my dreams and goals.
I like reviewing what I did the last year and looking at what worked
and what didn't. There's nothing like a clean slate. Almost like in school
when you start a new grade or a new semester. You're full of hope and
optimism because of the promise of an adventure of the unknown.

You probably feel like last year wasn't exactly what you wanted it to
be, but you can change the outcome for this year. Not only that but you
don't even have to wait until next year to start. I used to believe this to
be true. You might be thinking, "Well, it's already six months into the
year already, (insert date, etc) how can I change the outcome when half
of the year is gone?" I don't have a magic answer for that. All I know
is you could choose to look at the time that has been wasted, or you
could choose to look at all the time you have left to still make a difference. It doesn't matter if it's already December and you're reading this,
the point is, it doesn't matter how you start. It matters how you finish!
Let's say it is December. You could start putting forth your energy and

time into finishing out this year as strong as possible and then you will be setting yourself up for an amazing year next year!

Just as when a new year comes and you get the chance to start fresh, when you accept Christ as your savior, your old self passes away. You get the chance to let go of your old self so you can embrace the new, better version that is coming. Don't continue letting your past mistakes, faults and failures haunt you. Allow yourself to learn from them and then move on. We weren't meant to carry around a lot of spiritual "baggage".

Matthew 11:28
Come unto me, all ye that labor and are heavy laden,
and I will give you rest.

It's hard to rest when you're carrying around a lot of burdens. This is your time! This is when you can start beating that addiction or flush those bad habits. This can be the time when you get that promotion or tackle your next adventure. You deserve it. Go for it!

DAY 33

Jesus is Always More Than Enough

Psalm 23:5 b
Thou annointest my head with oil; my cup runneth over.

My cup runneth over. Spiritually, when we are thirsty and come to God, He usually doesn't just fill us back up, but He pours Himself into us so much that we overflow. He is not stingy with His blessings, mercy, grace, forgiveness, love, and every other good thing. I challenge you to think about how blessed you truly are. There are so many people out there that are less fortunate than us. We are not just a little blessed. We are running over with blessings.

When Jesus fed five thousand people with five loaves of bread and two fish, He more than met the needs of those people that day. Not only was everyone full, but there were twelve baskets full of leftovers!

When God answered Solomon's request for wisdom, He also gave Solomon everything else he didn't ask for! I'm sure there are plenty of other examples from the Bible but if God was willing to do this back then, what makes you think He wouldn't do it for you and me?

John 10:10
*The thief cometh not, but for to steal,
and to kill and to destroy: I am come that they might have life,
and that they might have it more abundantly.*

God wants us to be blessed abundantly and He is capable of doing so. So the next question is, are you capable of believing and receiving it?

Day 34

Best Friends

Proverbs 18:25
A man that hath friends must show himself friendly: and there is a friend that sticketh closer than a brother.

I'm sure we've all had best friends which we grew close to and then at some point they have drifted away. It could just have been that your lives were leading down different paths or whatever the case may be. That's not the kind of friendship I want to focus on. I want to focus on the type of friend that is in your life for more than a season. This type of friend is different. They are people who you know without a shadow of a doubt that God put them in your life for a reason. With them in your life, together, you are meant to do great things. You have a shared purpose. I want you to mentally evaluate the people in your life. Hopefully, somebody fitting this description has come to mind. Someone who you consider to be a part of your family. They have proven their love and loyalty to you time and time again.

One great example of this from the Bible is the friendship of David and Johnathan. On many occasions Johnathan put himself at risk by defying his father in order to help David. The words friend and family are words we use to describe people we love. When the proverb says: a friend that sticketh closer than a brother, it is implying a new, deeper bond for which, unless I'm mistaken, we don't have a word for. Because this type of person is more than a friend but not related by blood, and yet we have stronger bonds with them than some of our own family members. So, what is closer than this type of friend? Nothing.

I hope everyone has a friend like this. It makes a world of difference. An example for me in my life of this type of friend, is a married couple named Brad and Stephanie. I met them when I was 14 and in my freshman year of high school. This was a very confusing and difficult time of my life. I was still somewhat new at school because I had just moved to the area during the last half of my 8th grade year. I still didn't have many friends and didn't have much of a self image. I wasn't even really involved in anything until I decided to try out for the softball team. I still don't really know what possessed me to do it because I had never played softball a day in my life! Stephanie was the coach and Brad helped her train us. At the time, none of us knew Christ but something about them really stood out to me and I admired them a lot. Maybe it was because they taught me how to actually work hard at something and expected my best. They encouraged me and praised me when I performed well. They pushed me further than I thought was possible and as a result I actually became better. They seemed like they really cared and loved what they were doing. They had their work cut out with me but they were patient with me through the whole process of me learning.

Fast forward a little bit to when I was 16 years old. I was having major issues at home. My dad was deployed and my stepmother and I fought like cats and dogs. She actually had me arrested for something that wasn't entirely my fault, and she embellished the story quite a bit just to get me out of the house. I spent an entire month in jail and during my time there an older lady came to visit and hold a church service. I was mad at God and the entire world but I decided to hear this lady out. I desperately wanted to learn something new about God that I had never heard before because I was all out of hope. This lady taught me the reason Jesus died for the entire world and taught me what salvation was and for the first time in my life I finally understood what was missing in my life. I knew that I wanted to be saved and I needed to be saved. The church service ended with her leading me to Christ and me accepting Him as my savior. She also gave me a Bible that I read constantly for the remainder of my stay. I grew leaps and bounds while I was there because I would just talk to God all the time as if He were sitting in the cell with me. I began to believe my life had some sort of purpose and I knew He was going to get me out of jail. I remember asking Him not to let me go back home but to let me go to a school where I could learn more about Him. (Side note: God doesn't always answer our prayers the way we think He will because He certainly answered that prayer but it wasn't anything like I had in mind or would have chosen. However, for this period of time in my life, it was the best alternative.)

When my month was up I was enrolled in an all girls Christian Academy. Culture shock! Well I didn't have to live at home and I did learn a lot about God. I didn't want to be cut off from all my friends and family though, nor did I want to live in this home for girls with a bunch of strangers! Oh, well. I made the best of it and during my time there I remember being strongly advised never to speak to my old friends again once I left the home. I mean it was drilled into me. Almost like they were trying to brainwash me. I'm stubborn though and I fought it. I let it go in one ear and out the other. I remember thinking, "If salvation is so important, and I love my friends like I say I do, then surely they need to be saved too!" So, I did the only thing I could do. I prayed for my friends and family. I remember praying for a couple of girls I played softball with and then I especially remember praying for Brad and Stephanie. At times I felt foolish because I had no idea if my prayers were going to be answered and how. Also because here I was an hour and a half away and as the more time went on, I was sure I would just be forgotten. Sure, I had a reason to care about Brad and Stephanie. They were great examples to me, but part of me was afraid they wouldn't even remember me. Why should they? They helped coach lots of girls. I could have easily faded away into the background like all the others. So, why did I keep caring enough about them to pray for their salvation and for their marriage? All I know is that I just did care about them. I didn't want to get out of the girl's home and find out that they had gotten divorced. I loved them and I loved them together. They make an awesome team!

A year later I got my first visit back home. It was only a couple of days but I made the most of it. My sister had let me use her phone and I actually called a couple of my old friends from high school that I played softball with and had been praying for. I was scared to death but I witnessed to them anyway because I loved them enough to not care if I offended them or if they thought I was weird after that. And then on my last night, I stayed up for hours not caring if I lost sleep because I knew I was going back to the girl's home but I didn't know for how long and this was my last shot for a while. I stayed up past 3 or 4 in the morning writing a letter to Stephanie. I don't remember how long it was or what it said exactly, but I do know I told her about how I came to be saved and how important salvation was. I quoted a lot of scripture and let her know I had been praying for her and I loved her. I gave that letter to my sister to give to Stephanie when she went to school the next day. I was so afraid of the letter getting lost or discovered by my stepmom. If she discovered it, she would have confiscated it because she was following all the rules the director of the girls academy had given her. She made sure I didn't watch television and didn't have any communication with my old friends. (That she knew of) Like I said, I'm stubborn. It was especially hard not to just pop into the school that morning when we dropped my sister off before leaving and going back to the academy. I wanted nothing more at that moment in time than to run out of the vehicle and into the school to deliver my letter personally. But I knew I couldn't. So, I trusted my sister.

Fast forward again to shortly after I graduated from the academy and I was visiting at home again. I finally had the chance to talk to Stephanie on the phone and invited her over to our house for a bit after she got off work at the school. We stood in the yard and talked. We mostly talked about God and church and Christian books we had read.

I finally worked up the courage to ask her if she had gotten saved and she said yes. Then I asked if Brad had. She told me he did too! I was so happy! I knew there was no way she could know exactly how happy I was in that moment because she didn't know about the times I laid in bed unable to sleep because she had been on my heart and mind and so I prayed for her. Also, I don't really show my emotions that much.

As it turns out, Brad and Stephanie received Christ at a business/leadership conference they had attended. Just before my 20th birthday I ended up moving back in with my dad because he was separated from my stepmom and things were going south for me too and I needed some support. Plus, for some reason even unknown to me, in the back of my mind I was telling myself at least I would have some friends. I knew that Brad and Stephanie were Christians now, like I was and I was excited to have them be back in my life. More than that though. Looking back, I really believe God was whispering to me and telling me that I needed them back in my life. I know it was true because I could feel that it was true in my heart. And I knew for some reason I wanted them to play an active role in my life once again. I would even go as far as to say that I believe God let things in my life start falling apart so that I would move back in with my dad just so that I could get back around Brad and Stephanie. So, here I was, just getting ready to turn 20 and I got back in touch with Stephanie and wanted to get some time around her now that I had moved back to the area. I was still every bit of a misfit as I ever was with a very low self esteem. Stephanie just took me back under her wing like a big sister and poured love and positivity into me.

Shortly after that, Stephanie offered me an opportunity to what I thought was just a way to make some extra money. Sounded good to me. I had no money and no job. I got to attend conferences similar to the one she and Brad had attended and received Christ. I also got to meet some incredible people and I learned a lot of things that I wouldn't have learned anywhere else. I began to dream again and set goals for my future. I was inspired to work on myself and as a result my self-image improved drastically. Because of that opportunity she extended to me,

I gained the courage to pursue my dreams for my life. Including that of becoming a published author. There's no way I would have pursued that if it hadn't been for her and the positive environment she helped introduce me to. Today, Brad and Stephanie challenge me to grow in my faith as well as in every other area of my life. Even though now, we live at a distance from each other, they have still sacrificed a lot and been there for me when I needed them. Including the time when I was diagnosed with Type 1 Diabetes. I had been attending a conference with them in Peoria, Illinois and they literally saved my life. They took me to the emergency room because they noticed I was not myself and very weak. By this point I didn't even feel like walking and just talking made me feel out of breath. They stayed with me for at least 10 hours until my mom and my aunt could come and stay with me. I felt absolutely miserable and was in and out of it for most of that time but every time I would wake up, they were right there and I knew at that moment I wouldn't have wanted anyone else there with me.

I honestly don't know what my life would look like without their influence. I don't want to know. I wouldn't be half the person I am today and I probably wouldn't even be alive. I just know God put them in my life and for that I am eternally grateful!

DAY 35

Revenge

Romans 12:19

Dearly beloved, avenge not yourselves, but rather give place unto wrath: for it is written, vengeance is mine; I will repay, saith the Lord.

Because of our fallen nature, it is very natural for us to want to seek revenge when somebody has done us wrong. It could happen in many different forms. Maybe someone has stolen from you, lied to you, spread gossip about you, etc. I agree with you 100 percent that none of those things done to you were fair! Unfortunately, this is the world we live in and none of us can go through this life without experiencing some form of injustice.

I have witnessed the Lord work in my life concerning some people who have done wrong to me. I didn't seek revenge and in two pretty major instances that come to my mind, I can truly say I have come out better than the other individuals. Sometimes it takes a while for them to reap the harvest of their wrongful behavior they have sown but in due time it will come back to them. Today, in these two different situations, the individuals both live very hard, stressful lives and I would not want to trade places with them. I don't think God is through with them either because I believe when their time on this earth is finished, then they will be held fully accountable for their actions. The same is true for those who have wronged you. I believe what God can do to our transgressors is far worse than what you or I could do anyway.

Somehow, learning to let go and let God handle the situation gives me more peace in the end. Wouldn't peace of mind be worth it to you? I guarantee the other person would not have peace in their lives because I believe God keeps His promises. If you're still not sure, take a look at this verse:

Deuteronomy 32:35
To me belongeth vengeance, and recompense; their foot shall slide in due time: for the day of their calamity is at hand, and the things that shall come upon them make haste.

That kind of sounds to me like an inevitable doom for those people who do us harm. I would not want to have the Lord's judgement hanging over my head, following me around. Don't forfeit your blessings and peace by taking matters into your own hands. I believe if we do, we are taking that responsibility away from the Lord and then we place ourselves in a position where we are now deserving of the Lord's judgement. We will then find ourselves sharing the consequences with our offenders. Personally, I don't want to help shoulder their consequences because I have enough of my own mistakes to answer for one day. I cannot emphasize enough that it truly feels wonderful to let some things go and just watch God handle it. Those who have wronged you will lose their footing and before long it will be as if their lives will start to crumble around them.

Day 36

A.S.K
Ask
Seek
Knock

Matthew 7:7-8
Ask, and it shall be given you; seek, and ye shall find; knock and it shall be opened unto you: for everyone that asketh recieveth; and he that seeketh findeth, and to him that knocketh it shall be opened.

This is an encouraging passage of scripture. God could bless us with things we want before we even ask Him, but I believe He wants us to ask first. By asking Him, we admit that there is no other means of obtaining our desires. We are also placing our faith in Him that He will come through.

James 4:2 b
Ye have not because ye ask not.

We could think about something all day long. We could come up with plans to accomplish what we desire. We could talk about our dreams with other people but the reason you will still not have it is because you haven't asked God for it yet. Pray to God. Through your prayers you can knock at the gates of Heaven and they will be opened to you. Seek out the Lord and you will find Him. Ask Him for whatever you want or need and you will receive it.

One major reason why I believe that God operates this way is because He wants us to learn to rely on Him and not ourselves. Before I became a Christian and even for a while afterwards, it took me a while to comprehend that God was really the one providing for me all along. I used to think I was the one working, earning a living and paying my bills. Well, that's not entirely wrong. However, recently, I have learned that first and foremost God is the one who has given me a sound mind, and good health in order for me to go out and earn a living. In addition to that, every idea that comes to me so that I have something meaningful to write about has first been God's idea that He gave to me. Maybe the same is true for you. Maybe God has blessed you with certain abilities that you could use to further His cause.

Since realizing this, I have learned to depend on God more. I have learned not to stress out about things as much because God has never failed me before and He's not going to start now. In addition to that, I have become more confident in who I am and in pursuing my callings in my life. Over the past few years I have truly started believing I am worthy of the best in life and that has helped me to have the courage to ask God for help in providing more for me and the faith that He will follow through with His promises. When I pray and ask for more, I can see opportunities for me everywhere I look. God is opening doors for me all around me. He is willing to do the same for you too!

DAY 37

The Enemy of My Enemy Is My Friend

John 15:15

Henceforth I call you not servants; for the servant knoweth not what his Lord doeth: but I have called you friends; for all things that I have heard of my Father I have made known unto you.

My enemy is ruthless and pure evil. He is cunning and controlling. He had me blinded and in bondage. He had me brainwashed to enforce his agenda. I was his slave. He has billions if not billions more, all of which he cares nothing about. He is so good at what he does that I didn't even know he was my enemy. He can fool you into believing that he is your friend and will act like he has your best interests in mind, but that's not actually the case. He has his real motives kept secret. He is a royal prince but he doesn't own a castle. He owns the world. His name is Satan.

This enemy of mine also has another enemy. His other enemy is God. God is greater and mightier than Satan. God rescued me from the hands of the Evil one. I never knew true love until God, the King of Heaven and all of creation passed by my way. Matter of fact, He came looking for me and broke the chains that held me in bondage. He removed the blinders from my eyes. He cleansed me and made me whole. My enemy is no match for my Redeemer.

The enemy of my enemy is many things to me. He is my father and my commander in battle. He is my provider and my protector. He is the example I pattern my life after. He is my shepherd, making sure I don't get lost. He is my savior. Most of all, when nobody else was, I'm glad He was and always will be my friend.

DAY 38

Do Get Your Hopes Up

Psalm 31:24
Be of good courage, and he shall strengthen your heart,
all ye that hope in the Lord.

*I*f you're like me, someone at some point in your life has told you to not get your hopes up about something. True, life is unpredictable. You may not make the sports team in high school. You may not get accepted into your first choice for college. Life has a lot of competitions based on performance. You want to climb the corporate ladder. The problem with that is, so does everyone else. There are others who want that promotion and will do anything in order to get it. Including playing dirty and taking advantage of others. Sometimes just working your guts out isn't enough.

Growing up, and still quite a lot today, I receive advice to not get my hopes up about something. When I was younger I thought that was sound advice. However, what I didn't realize was by adopting that attitude, I was accepting a negative outlook and I was setting myself up for failure. As time would go on, I found myself believing that I was unworthy of the things I really wanted and I became discouraged from even trying to pursue my passions anymore because if I got my hopes up only to be let down again I would be crushed, so why even try anymore? At best, I could only hope to be average with my life.

What's wrong with average? There's successful, average, and unsuccessful. Average is right in the middle. Successful is hot, average is lukewarm, unsuccessful is cold. It's kind of like beverages that are best served hot. (I could use coffee as an example but I personally don't like coffee and never drink it so I don't know that it's good hot or not.) We'll use soup as an example. Soup tastes the best when it's hot. When it gets to be about room temperature….eh it's ok but not the greatest and then when it becomes cold ugh. Better warm it back up right? Anybody else agree? Average is like room temperature soup. It's not exciting. In fact it's dull and boring. When your soup is cold you're more likely moved to action to heat it back up. Likewise in life if you're unhappy with your circumstances, (on the unsuccessful side of the equation) chances are you will be moved to do something about it. You will want to change your circumstances and seek happiness and fulfillment in order to get to the successful side. The problem is, a majority of people are stuck in average. Their soup is lukewarm. They rationalize. It's not so bad. Really? You're comfortable in average because you are given just enough to keep living comfortably. Sure, you realize it could be better but it could also be worse so you become happy with where you are. Then, you find yourself stuck there. The longer you live in average, the harder it is to get out. Eventually, you will become unhappy because your life will pass you by and one day you will look back and think, "Where did my time go?" "Have I really not accomplished anything with my life?" By settling for average you give up your dreams and you don't even realize it. Living with nothing to motivate you and keep you going is in my opinion, a foundation for a sad, boring and frustrating existence.

Now, I have come to understand the negativity in mediocrity. Being told not to get my hopes up is some of the worst advice I've ever received and I cringe every time I hear it. I have made it a habit to look at situations from all angles, so I realize when people give me this advice it is given with good intentions. The individual is subtly warning me not to count on something going favorably because if it doesn't work out, I'll get disappointed. In other words, prepare for the worst outcome, just in case so you don't get hurt. Regardless of the good intent to protect me, it is still bad advice. Personally, I have trained myself to refuse to prepare for the worst. There are numerous verses in the Bible where God promises to answer prayers. That alone should be enough to give you new hope. That is why I can hope and expect the best outcomes in my life no matter the situation. God wants us to hope and place our hopes and dreams in Him. I want to live my life like Psalm 71: 14 – But I will hope continually, and I will yet praise thee (God) more and more.

Never cease to place your hope in the Lord, for as long as He is here, (which is always) there will always be a reason to hope.

Are You Prepared for Battle?

1 Peter 5:8

Be sober, be vigilant; because your adversary the devil, as a roaring lion, walketh about, seeking whom he may devour:

I'm sure you may have heard it said that we are in a spiritual war. You and I are soldiers in God's army. We have an enemy to fight. That enemy is Satan. He is constantly trying to trip us up, destroy us and deceive us. He is ruthless in his attacks and never stops to rest or take a break. Likewise, neither should we. Read Ephesians 6: 10-18. That passage describes the armor we should wear in battle. Never take it off. Keep it polished. Repair the weak spots in it. There are six essential pieces that make up your armor.

1) The belt of truth. This is the base of your armor. The first piece you put on. It is your knowledge of God's word and it helps hold the other pieces of armor in place.
2) The breastplate of righteousness. The breastplate protects your heart. Keep your heart righteous. Don't let it be exposed to any threat.
3) Shoes of the gospel of peace. Many times the truth from the Bible is referenced as a foundation upon which we need to stand because it is firm and solid. Our feet are important because we need them in order to stand. We also use them to walk which

is why we need them protected. Shoes don't just cover the top of our feet but also provide a barrier between our feet and the ground. Stepping on rough terrain without protection could cripple us and take us out of the fight. We use our shoes to advance forward. Where our feet go so do our shoes. Having our feet protected by the gospel of peace not only benefits us but also those who need our help. We bring with us the good news of Jesus Christ on our feet because it is the most effective in helping us keep our balance and stand our ground.

4) The shield of faith. You use a shield to hide behind. You keep it out in front of you to take blows instead of taking on blows directly. It protects you and gives you courage because it provides some peace of mind to know you're not too vulnerable. Keep your faith out in front of you. It will do the protecting and give you the courage you need.

5) The helmet of salvation. Protect your mind with the knowledge of your salvation. Keep it in the forefront of your mind. Knowing you are saved and will be kept safe provides confidence.

6) The sword of the spirit. The word of God, the Bible is your sword. Use it to attack the enemy. When Satan attacks you with lies, combat him with a verse of scripture. The truth is stronger.

Lastly, we are instructed to pray. Without prayer, our armor is ineffective. Sometimes in a battle you might be separated from everyone else and surrounded by the enemy. In those instances, pray for yourself, but also pray for your brothers and sisters in Christ because they are also in the war. Now picture yourself in your mind about to enter the war, fully adorned in all your armor. You would be careful to forget nothing because deep down you have a certain respect for the enemy. That respect is necessary because you have to acknowledge the fact that he is dangerous. That's why you suit up! You know he has potential to cause you harm and he certainly will! He will not go easy on you because you forgot your helmet. He will actually see your weak point and focus his attacks on your head. Without your breastplate, your chest becomes a direct target! Knowing how dangerous he is, why would you want to take off any piece of your armor? Likewise, why would you want it to become weakened by neglecting it? Keep your sword sharpened. Don't allow yourself to get dull on your scripture. Keep it fresh in your life. Don't let your helmet and breastplate get rusty. Keep them polished. Your mind and heart needs to stay pure. When your feet start to slip and your shoes get dirty, brush them off. Find solid ground. Keep pressing forward. Somebody needs you. Repair your shield of faith when the enemy scratches it up and takes chunks out of it. Reinforce your belt when it gets frayed or starts to slip. I realize you are not at war every moment of your life. You will have times to rest. You will have moments of victory and "mountaintop" experiences where everything is good in your life. However, your sword and armor should always be ready when trouble does come to your door again because it inevitably will.

DAY 40

Being A Cheerful Giver

2 Corinthians 9:7
Every man according as he purposeth in his heart, so let him give; not grudgingly, or of necessity: for God loveth a cheerful giver.

Whenever I think about this verse or the subject in general, one person always comes to mind. Her name is Jeanette. I met her during a critical and very confusing time in my life. She sort of took me under her wing and "adopted" me as a granddaughter. I met her when I was about 16 and for the next 4 years she played a very influential role in my life. At first being in her presence was a little intimidating because I had never met someone who was always cheerful, loving, and giving. She was so selfless. I never saw her get tired of serving other people. She never thinks of herself. There were times when I wondered how she could keep doing it all when even she didn't have that much.

Over time we forged a special bond. I truly believe the Lord placed her in my life. I learned many things from her. I found myself enjoying being in her presence. Whether we were cleaning the church or running to the grocery store, I was happy to tag along and help out. I think also, another reason why I was drawn to her was because she used to always tell me that I was created to do great things with my life. I didn't really believe her but it was nice to hear it anyways because I never had someone tell me that before. I just felt average and like I didn't really have a purpose.

Sunday afternoons after the morning church service was always the best time. All of Jeanette's family and occasionally some friends from church would come over to her house and eat lunch. In all honesty this was THE place to be because Jeanette would go all out and literally prepare a feast! She is an amazing cook and would have been working on preparing everything the night before and a little in the morning before church so that everyone could just come over as soon as church was out and be ready to eat. I really felt special being invited over to eat because I felt accepted and like I was a part of the family since I was away from my family. There was no way I would go hungry if she was around!

In addition to that, she would just always buy something for somebody because she knew they needed it. She never thought twice about it. I have even been on the receiving end of her generosity. There was a period of time where I attended college in Tennessee and she sent me a care package every month while I was away. Just the fact that she thought of me meant a great deal to me. I have often wondered how she managed to do it all. Staying up late and waking up early, serving people all day long. She never seemed tired and never complained. I know now it's because she has a servant's heart. She's truly a godly example of an amazing woman that I can only hope to be like one day.

One last thing. She has never told me this, but someone else had. I don't know if it's true but apparently Jeanette told someone that the first time she saw me, she heard God tell her that she needed to help me. That she was supposed to be there to guide me for whatever I needed. She didn't know what that would be but she definitely fulfilled that. I really don't know if it is true but a part of me likes to believe that it is because I believe everyone I have ever met was for a reason. I believe God has put certain people in my life for a reason. If anyone could hear God speak to their heart it would be Jeanette. She just has such a huge heart and is so wise and so in tune with God.

I know life gets crazy and after I moved away I dropped the ball in staying in communication with you but this is one of my simple ways of thanking you for everything you have done for me! One little tiny way I can think of giving back to you and hopefully being a blessing to you for a change! I love you Mawmaw!

DAY 41

Quicksand

Psalm 40:2
*He brought me up also out of a horrible pit, out of the miry clay,
and set my feet upon a rock, and established my goings.*

love this verse because it so accurately describes my life before receiving Christ as my savior. Spiritually, I was sort of in quicksand. I felt like my life was a complete wreck. True I was only 16 but I hated everything about my life. I literally had nothing that I enjoyed or looked forward to everyday. I remember times when I would go to sleep and just want so badly to not wake up the next day. And then, every day I would wake up again and I would be disappointed. I was so unhappy. So many things were out of my control that I didn't know how to fix them or when I tried fixing things about myself it wouldn't work. It seemed like the more I tried to improve my life, the worse it would get. The faster I struggled, the faster I would sink. I had pretty much given up hope for my life. I no longer pictured my future because I didn't want there to be one. As bad as things were I couldn't see how they could ever get better.

Until the day someone explained some biblical truths to me that nobody else had ever taken the time to do. The things she said to me resonated with my heart and spoke to my soul. I knew what she was saying was true. Just as all hope was almost abandoned I called on Jesus for help. I asked Him to save me because I realized I needed His help.

Not only that but I truly wanted Him to be a part of my life. I was tired of everyone else letting me down. I was finally ready to try trusting God for once. Completely broken and hopeless, I felt as if Jesus had wrapped His arms around me. Something in my heart changed that day. And it felt as if a literal weight had been lifted off my shoulders. I knew I had been carrying around a lot of baggage. Self loathing, every worry in the world, every sin I had ever committed. All of it up to that point was erased and taken off my shoulders. I felt so light as if I could stand much taller and even float a little even though my feet didn't leave the ground.

Jesus is our rock and our solid foundation. When He is the foundation for our life we can build a strong and stable life upon Him. He established my goings when He saved me. As long as we have Him we can never go wrong or lose our way again. He is our guide through life. As long as we stand on Him, the Bible we need not worry about falling in anymore quicksand pits the world has hidden from view. The world and the Devil will lie to you to try and get you to take a path that will lead you to making careless decisions that could have been avoided. Decisions that will have consequences that could cause you to fall into another quicksand pit and be stuck dealing with for a long time afterwards. I'll be the first to admit I'm not perfect, nor is my life because I'm human too and make mistakes several times every day. However, I have tried my best to remain true to a lot of my standards and beliefs. With that being said, even though my life isn't where I thought it would be, I have to admit in a lot of ways it is better than I could have hoped it would be if I tried to wing it on my own. I know God has helped me through every step of the way and I also give credit to my close friends and family that God has given me to help guide me.

DAY 42

YOUnique

Psalm 139:14a
I will praise thee for I am fearfully and wonderfully made:

For most of my life I walked around believing I was an accident. I thought I was alive merely by chance. Therefore I believed that I had no purpose and that life in itself was meaningless. If my life had no point then what was the point of life at all? When I was blind and believed these things to be true, I was a slave to confusion and depression. I used to dwell on circumstances that were beyond my control. Things such as had my mother and father never met, I wouldn't exist. Or what if my grandparents had never married each other and had married other people instead? It really can seem as if our lives are a result of such a thin thread of opportunity. If things hadn't happened exactly the way they did where would we be? Could it have altered the course of our life that much or would it be the difference in not existing at all? Because of these thoughts I felt worthless. I struggled to find a place in life and I felt empty inside.

Now, as a Christian, God has helped me to believe the opposite. To be completely honest, it has taken me a while to believe that I am in fact here on this earth for a purpose. Not only that but I am alive at the perfect time that God has chosen for me to be alive. I was born at just the right moment and will accomplish great things during my lifetime that God has assigned for me to do. Things that nobody else but I can accomplish. God specifically designed me the way that I am and He makes no mistakes. I am perfect in His sight and He has been in control of everything from the beginning.

I know I am valuable and if these things are true for me then I know they are true for you too. There will never be another you. Don't waste your life hating who you are. Also, stop comparing yourself to others because wishing you were like someone else is wasting yourself and who God intended you to be. It hasn't been easy for me to accept myself or to figure out that what I thought were weaknesses were actually my strengths. I had tried to be someone else for so long that it took time for me to discover who I truly was and how special I was. I'm guessing there have been times where you have felt the same way. Not only did I have a lot to discover about myself, I also had to learn to be comfortable with who I was and at peace with that. Slowly, over time, was I able to project some of my newfound confidence onto the outside of me whenever I was in public. I could openly voice my opinions in front of others without fear of criticism. I could appreciate others for their individuality. I would become less offended by others behavior or things they would say. Maybe you will experience some victory in these areas as well. Hopefully you can start to see yourself the way God sees you and start to love yourself the way God loves you!

He Must Increase

John 3:30
He must increase but I must decrease.

One thing that I like about the Bible is that it teaches us things that are completely opposite from what the world will try to teach you. Before I became a Christian I was miserable because I was taking the world's advice. Advice that kept changing or had different applications to different situations. As an example for today's verse, let's apply it to the topic of success. The world will tell you that in order to be successful, you need to take advantage of other people, lift up yourself and put others down. In other words, step on them and fight your way to the top. Maybe you could take credit for another individual's work or maim their character. You could be tempted to do whatever it took to climb one more rung up that ladder to success.

Deep down everyone wants to succeed. However, everybody's definition of success might look a little bit different from someone else's. For some, success is purely monetary. For others, it may be the perfect career, spouse, home or family or any combination of these. People dedicate a majority of their lives trying to accomplish these things in order to obtain that picture of success that hangs in their minds' eye. What do you want? How would you define success? What keeps you awake at night? What do you see when you close your eyes? What is the first and last thing you think of everyday? If you truly want to make your dreams of success come true, the best way to do that is to do the opposite of what the world tells you. If you want to succeed, the best way to do so is by humbling yourself. Try putting God first and making Him #1 in your life.

James 4:10
Humble yourselves in the sight of the Lord, and He shall lift you up.

Are there people who have succeeded in corporate America who have lied and cheated their way to the top? Absolutely. I'm willing to bet though, that not everyone is guaranteed success if they choose to go that route. Perhaps it is easier for most because of our sinful nature. It most definitely is easier to do wrong than to do right. My guess is because we can't see the results those choices bring because it usually takes a little while before they catch up with us. But let me tell you, it's the same way with doing the right things. It might be harder to do right, and the positive results you seek could be a long way off in the future. What about peace of mind? Wouldn't that alone be worth it initially? Otherwise you know what you did was wrong and you know you lied during your interview, so now you have to live with that on your conscience. What about when your coworker left the room and your boss assumed you decided to go the extra mile and cleaned the break room without being told, so since he already assumed it was your idea you didn't bother to tell him it was really someone else's idea?

I believe even the little situations could all play a key role in helping you acquire what you want. I also believe in the law of reaping and sowing. Sow bad seeds and you will reap bad seeds. Sow good seeds and you will reap good seeds. Your harvest will come up from places you have never imagined. God can open doors of opportunity for you in only the way God operates. He loves to bless us and surprise us. It all depends on the type of seed you have been planting. I believe when you make a habit of humbling yourself to God, He works on you and prepares you to be able to handle the greater things He has in store for you. It's as simple as that, friends. The way up is down!

DAY 44

Resist!

James 4:7 b
Resist the Devil and he will flee from you.

For many years I avoided confrontation. It is uncomfortable confronting others with a problem you may have with them. However, I have learned that it's better to resolve the problem than to cower in fear behind it by not addressing it. The same can be said about voicing your opinion. It's hard to put your opinion out there when it's not popular and everyone else thinks differently than you do. By conditioning yourself to constantly submit to others it becomes ten times harder to stand up for what's right when a really important issue surfaces. When you choose to not voice your opinion or when you choose not to confront someone, you are really giving up your power. I used to believe I was just keeping the peace and trying not to rock the boat. In retrospect, by trying to keep the peace, I was forfeiting my peace. Maybe that particular conversation ended peacefully for someone else but it was at the expense of my own peace! Haven't you ever held back in a conversation and wished later that you had spoken up? Now, you're not at peace because your lack of courage is bothering you.

We're not supposed to bow down or roll over belly up to the enemy and surrender. We are told to resist! When the Devil attacks, fight back! I love the end result. He will flee! Not sometimes he will flee.

Not possibly he will flee. When he realizes you're serious and you call his bluff, every time he will flee because he knows he can't really harm you. He knows he has no real power over you and he can't control you, therefore he can't win. The only power he has over you is the power you give him. He's just trying to intimidate you by getting in your face and roughing you up a bit, but it only works if you let him. I hope by now you are beginning to see that you hold more power than you realize. Stop being afraid and start utilizing that power. With God's help, you are unstoppable!

DAY 45

Out of My Way

Luke 4:8
And Jesus answered and said unto him,
Get thee behind me, Satan: for it is written,
Thou shalt worship the Lord thy God, and him only shalt thou serve.

The focus for this verse is "Get thee behind me, Satan." I love this phrase and I love reading about how the devil tries to tempt Jesus. For one thing, I can't believe he was dumb enough to try. He knew full well that Jesus was the son of God and therefore perfect. So, why bother? Perhaps because it is so deeply rooted in his DNA that he just can't accept the facts. He just can't face the music and come to grips that he is a loser and will always be a loser. And so, he attempts to get Jesus to sin. Jesus saw straight through Satan's tricks and just like Jesus we are meant to plow right through Satan too.

I understand why Satan tries tempting us because we are more gullible. However, I believe it's your fault if you stay gullible. There is tons of information at your disposal to educate yourself spiritually. The sooner you learn to recognize his tricks and get quicker at thwarting him the quicker you can have your victory. When we thwart his plans we leave him behind in the dust. Once Satan is behind us, he is out of sight and out of mind. Don't misunderstand. I'm not downplaying the fact that he is a real threat. There are times when he needs to be on our minds and addressed because whatever issues he's causing shouldn't be ignored.

The rest of the time, we shouldn't dwell on him because having him ruling in our minds only glorifies him. He loves attention, honor and glory. Dwelling on him is a form of worship. Maybe you don't mean to because you didn't realize it. Well, now you can change that.

I believe also that not every spiritual battle or every trial or tribulation needs to be fought with prayer and counsel. Before I lose you, stay with me. I'm not belittling prayer by any means or whatever you may be going through. Let's just say you struggle with negative thoughts about yourself. That is a real battle. It's something I struggle with almost daily. But I don't need to crack open my Bible or ask God what He thinks every time I think this way. I know how God feels about me and I have learned to recognize that Satan is the one behind all negative thoughts that enter my mind. So all I have to do is dismiss these thoughts as soon as they arrive. In other words I'm telling Satan to shut up, get out of my mind and get out of my way. Sometimes it really is that simple. Don't over complicate it. Even if it feels like you are all alone in this, because the Devil likes it when you feel this way, just know that you're not. You always have God with you and I'm here with you. The devil wants to isolate us and make us feel like we're the only one who knows what it's like to face whatever your circumstances might be. Hello....? Are you forgetting he's the biggest liar to ever walk the face of the earth??? I hope you're ready to link arms with me and get quicker at claiming your victories. Let's deny the devil any honor and glory. Whenever he gets in our way, may we boldly proclaim, just as Jesus did, "Get thee behind me, Satan."

DAY 46

Things I Wish I Knew Growing Up

Jeremiah 1:5
Before I formed thee in the belly I knew thee;
and before thou camest forth out of the womb I sanctified thee,
and I ordained thee a prophet unto the nations.

Have you ever wondered what your life would be like if you knew certain things when you were younger? I have several times. My life as a teenager was very hard because I was empty inside. I was trying to fill a void inside myself which at times caused me to rebel. I was angry, confused and didn't feel loved. Thankfully, I can pass on to my future children what I know so they won't have to feel the same way. Throughout my journey with God over the last almost 12 years I have learned a lot. So much that it is hard to narrow it down and choose which have meant the most to me. I could go on about faith, success, facing your fears, leadership, personal development, how to have confidence in myself, all of which are super important topics. I think I have it contained to about three subjects though.

1) I wish I had known that I was not on earth by mistake. My self confidence was at an all time low because I believed I was born by accident. This is where the verse Jeremiah 1:5 comes into play. Just as God knew what He was doing with me while I was still

developing in my mother's womb, God knew what He was planning on doing with you also. Not one of us is here by mistake. Not only are we designed exactly the way we were meant to be, we each have a unique path that only God has intended for us to walk. We each have our own unique purposes for our lives.

2) I wish I knew the importance of salvation, the reason for it and why I needed it. I remember a time when I was scared of death. I didn't know that I would go to Heaven if I died. Thinking back, I can remember lies from the Devil saying that I would go to Heaven because I hadn't done anything really bad like kill someone. It was like there were certain degrees of bad that determined whether or not you went to Heaven. So I bought into that believing if I at least kept trying to do good then all of that would outweigh the bad. But for some reason I still wasn't sure. I didn't know what Ephesians 2:8 says. "For by grace are ye saved through faith; and that not of yourselves: it is a gift of God: Not of works, lest any man should boast." I didn't know I needed salvation just because of the fact that I was a sinner. Romans 3:23- "For all have sinned, and come short of the glory of God. " When you don't feel loved, it's hard to believe you're special and that God really loves you. There has to come a time when you believe it otherwise there would be no need for John 3:16- " For God so loved the world, that he gave his only begotten son, that whosoever believeth in him should not perish, but have everlasting life."

3) Lastly, I wish I had known the twofold command God gives to children and parents found in Ephesians 6:1-4. As children, God expects us to obey our parents and promises us a long life. As parents, God expects us to raise our children in the nurture and admonition of the Lord. He also tells us not to provoke our children to wrath. Growing up, I wasn't raised in the nurture and admonition of the Lord. As I got older and rebelled, I wish I knew it wasn't completely my fault. It was because of

poor parenting and not just because I was a horrible child like I was made to believe. A lot of times I rebelled was because I was provoked by a step parent who truly didn't have my best interests in mind. There were times when I recognized that certain parenting procedures were ridiculous and I knew I secretly enjoyed rebelling because I had been hardened to the point of not caring so much about my repercussions. I'm just saying there were times when I might have taken more responsibility than I should have and I wish I had not beaten myself up so much. If I could talk to the 16 year old me who struggled to find things to enjoy about life and who didn't even know why she was still alive and who had absolutely no idea how incredible life was going to be in the future, I would tell her these three things. Then, I would say, "Keep your chin up. The 28 year old you is absolutely rocking at life. Have a little bit more fun while you still can and are not so burdened down with responsibility and bills. I'll see ya again in 12 years, winner!"

DAY 47

Are You Afraid of Failing?

Proverbs 24:16
For a just man falleth seven times, and riseth up again:
but the wicked shall fall into mischief.

'm willing to bet as you were growing up, you fell a few times while learning to walk. My guess is, you fell off your bike a few times too! Surely over the course of your life, you have fallen more than seven times. Every time you have fallen, you got back up. How come you don't just stay on the ground? Haven't you gotten tired of falling and making a fool of yourself? Haven't you had enough of getting hurt from falling down? I've never seen anyone stay on the ground and say, "Just leave me here. At least this way I can't fall again and get hurt!" No! This is because you're not a failure! Only a failure would refuse to get back up.

Now, that we've established that you're not a failure, what else are you afraid of failing at? Maybe, like myself, you are afraid of going after what you really want and trying your best to achieve it, and you still fall short of obtaining it? Well, one thing is for sure. You most definitely will fail if you don't try. So by trying to avoid failing, you automatically fail. Brilliant idea! NOT! Have you ever considered what would happen if you went all in and tried to obtain what you want and you actually succeeded? Now, that's an idea! So, why do we let our fear of failure keep us from even attempting to fulfill our dreams and goals? You don't even know you're going to fail unless you try. Even if you do try and fail, it isn't the end of the world. You figure out what didn't work, then you adjust and try again. If there's anything I've learned about success it's that failing is how you succeed. If you fail enough times, you will eventually succeed. It all depends on how many times you're willing to stand back up and go for it again.

I love learning about success stories of well known people who failed their way to success because it motivates me to know all my failures are temporary too. For example, Dr. Seuss was turned down by publishers 27 times! However, he believed in his dream of writing children's books so much that he couldn't give up on it. Some of my favorite childhood books were <u>Green Eggs and Ham,</u> and <u>The Cat in the Hat.</u> It took Thomas Edison 10,000 tries and over 10 years to create a working light bulb. Could you stick with something for 10 years even though people would probably think you're crazy? It's not a matter of IF you will succeed but WHEN you will succeed. The only way you will be a failure is if you live your whole life and never accomplish any of your dreams and goals before you die. Once you die, you're out of time. While you are still living, you still have seeds of greatness in you. What are you going to do with them?

There's not a single excuse in the world that can actually hold you back unless you let it. You have more power over your life and your future than you think you do. I believe there's not a single person on earth who has ever been born or who will be born who is destined for failure. The only person destined for failure is the devil. The truth of the matter is that he knows it too! He knows he's going to lose to God. He even knew full well that Jesus is the son of God when he tried tempting Jesus in the wilderness. So, if the devil can still make attempts at success when he knows he's going to fail no matter what, can you take that chance and possibly succeed in the process? Can you move to that new location or start a new job and believe that the right doors of opportunity will open for you along the way? Your success is just out of your reach but it is totally obtainable. I say just go for it!

DAY 48

Are You In A Box?

Matthew 5:16
*Let your light so shine before men, that they may see your good works
and glorify your Father which is in Heaven.*

Somehow when I was growing up, I just knew I was different. I liked reading sometimes at recess while the other kids played. I dreamed of being an author because in my mind that meant I had achieved something worthwhile. Even in high school my teachers would try to help me map out my future based on my strengths. I always heard that on average, people who were good at English were also good at History. On the other side of the equation, people who were good at Math were generally good at Science. Once again, I didn't quite fit into their "box". I was good at English and Science and terrible at Math and History. I think my guidance counselors gave up on me because nothing they suggested seemed right for me. I didn't fit in any category. Not to mention I didn't see "become a published author and make millions of dollars" anywhere on their list of options for me to choose from. In the back of my mind, I knew that could be an option for me. I just didn't have the self-confidence or any idea how I could achieve it. So, I kept that dream hidden in the bottom of my heart.

I lived several years after graduation just going with the flow. I took other people's advice on what I should do with my life. I was just a square peg trying to fit into a round hole and it just honestly wasn't working. Oh, sure, on the outside I was Miss Chameleon. I could change and adapt to my surroundings because that's part of surviving. On the inside, I was slowly, agonizingly, dying. I was miserable because I knew I wasn't living up to my full potential. I knew I wasn't fulfilling my purpose in life. I was also afraid. Living in my box was at times comfortable and easy. Until it's not. What's comfortable or easy about reporting to a job that makes you want to cry every day because you know you have to go since you have no other option at this point? What's comfortable about knowing the only person you can blame is yourself because you were too scared to step out and pursue your calling before your work life became that bad? There's nothing easy about reminding yourself that you should have had that problem fixed before it happened. Even if there were no circumstances that made life difficult for you, (ex: no debt, no health issues, no crummy job) what's comfortable about having that tugging on your heart or the thought pop up in your mind over and over to chase after that dream or goal? It's not at all easy being painfully aware that you have wasted another day of your life.

For me, having the dream of becoming a published author was a fire burning inside me that would not be extinguished. I know somebody reading this knows this feeling. That's because whatever it is, it's your purpose, or at least a part of it. You have a light within you that is meant to shine and be shared with the world! By you succeeding at whatever it is, you will bring honor and glory to God who created you and who gave you your dreams and desires. Stop trying to fit into the box the world wants to put you in. Boxes will lure you with their false sense of security, but boxes aren't really made to keep you safe. They're made to keep you contained. To make sure your light doesn't shine. To make sure you don't achieve success. Being trapped in a box will keep you from helping anybody and will keep you from being happy. It's time to climb out of the box!

DAY 49

Zombies Are Real

Proverbs 29:18 a
Where there is no vision, the people perish:

*I*s there anyone reading this who loves a good zombie movie like I do? I mean, I liked them even before they were really popular. Even though they scared me silly. Every little noise outside in the dark could be the shuffling of a zombie nearby. You know what I'm talking about. You have to hurry up and get in your car and shut the door as quickly as possible! How about that popular show on Netflix, The Walking Dead? Not gonna lie, I got hard core hung up on that show too. Let me just put it this way. Whenever I'm really bored, I love letting my imagination run rampant and my favorite scenarios are end of the world, zombie apocalypse type of circumstances. I'm weird, I know. It's gonna be ok, I promise, I have a point! You guys, I even have dreams about this stuff!

Just recently, I dreamed I was stuck in a school bus full of other people who were trying to seek shelter from zombies. These zombies were kinda smart too. There were so many of them and they were so strong that they started flipping the school bus over and over to try and bust out all the windows. Well, they did, and since I was just small enough, I could climb out of one of the windows. I ran like nobody's business to the nearest house where I was safe up until the point where I woke up.

Ok, granted, I know there is not rotting corpses walking around trying to eat you. However, I do believe that you can be 100% alive and also be 100% dead on the inside. These type of people are the ones who are zombies in today's world. A zombie is someone who has given up on their dreams and goals for their lives. In other words, they have lost their vision and settled for the path of least resistance. When that happened, they died on the inside. Can you guess what they eat? They eat your goals and dreams! They couldn't accomplish theirs, so you better believe they're going to try to eat yours so that you will be just like them! A zombie is that nosey neighbor who scoffs at your goal of being debt free. A zombie is that annoying relative who says," I know someone who tried that and it doesn't work." I can spot a zombie a mile away. They're usually dragging their feet on their way into work Monday morning. Or they give themselves away by the first words that come out of their mouths. Zombies are negative people. They sometimes carry themselves in a defeated manner. Sort of like, well, this is my life and this is as good as it is going to get.

Other zombies are hard to spot because on the outside, they appear to be happy and successful. That's because they don't even know they're dead on the inside. They have fooled themselves for so long and now they're fooling you. Ok, so maybe you're Mr. Bigshot where you work. Do you really expect me to believe that when you were growing up, you didn't want to be an astronaut or a fire fighter or a fill in the blank? So, somewhere along the way you settled for your current job because it was close to home with a decent wage. You also want me to believe that you actually enjoy reporting to said job all the while helping to build someone else's dream and help them make tons of money…? Rrright… (I hope you can hear the sarcasm in my voice.) When you encounter zombies like this, don't let them infect you with their rotten mentality. You don't have to settle in any area of your life. You deserve for your dreams to come true. It's not always going to be easy. You're going to have to fight for your dreams and at times fight off the zombies. Other times it is completely appropriate to run away from them! You need to protect your dreams from people who don't understand them and who do not hesitate to question you or belittle you for being a dreamer and a goal planner. We are living in a zombie apocalypse. The vast majority of people today do what they think is smart and safe vs. what they actually want. Which side of the equation do you fall on? Have you become like a zombie? Are you living everyday without meeting your purpose, drained of any passion for your life?

DAY 50

The Magnetism of Mediocrity

Romans 8:28
*And we know that all things work together for good to them that love
God, and to them who are the called according to his purpose.*

I remember a time in my life when I used to actually tell people that I wanted to live an average, normal life. That thought process came from the belief that I didn't have a purpose for my life. I didn't believe that I would do anything meaningful with my life. Honestly, just as much as I believed that, I hoped that it was true. I didn't want to believe that I could make a difference because it kind of scared me. It meant I would have to be this wonderfully successful person who "had it all together." I didn't know how I would get there and the idea was intimidating. The irony of it all though, is I'm still far away from that image in my mind of a wonderful, successful person, and I definitely don't "have it all together." However, I do believe now that I have a purpose. I'm trying harder than ever to fulfill that purpose every day. Yes, it still scares me and is very intimidating. Even worse is the feeling of relentless misery that haunts me each day that I don't actively pursue my purpose. With that being said, ultimately, my fears and doubts get driven away.

In addition, I think one of the hardest things to do when it comes to pursuing your purpose, is to step away from mediocrity. I really believe there is a sort of magnetism to mediocrity. The reason I say that is because for the most part, we are trained our entire lives to prepare ourselves for an average life. We are taught to go to school, get good grades, get a good job and work until we retire. That might be helpful if that will get you where you truly want to go in life. That just doesn't have to be your only option. For me, I remember daydreaming of being a published author when I was a kid. As I got older, I kept that dream hidden deep in my heart. I knew I didn't need to go to college to "learn how to write." I think writing is a gift and it isn't something that can be entirely taught. The same can be said with a gift you might possess. Maybe you're naturally funny and want to be a comedian. Maybe you can sing and enjoy playing instruments. If those are your dreams, you should pursue them. You won't develop those gifts by sitting in a classroom. Sure, I get it. You do have bills to pay and your dreams aren't exactly providing the lifestyle you want. There's nothing wrong with working long enough so you can fund your dream until it does become a reality. Just don't let yourself get trapped and lose your dream. I honestly think that happened to me for a period of time. I got comfortable for a while at a factory I used to work at. I remember a time when I actually enjoyed working there. I could have easily stayed there longer until just showing up became not so easy. During the Summer I probably worked 6 days a week for up to four months at a time. I showed up for work at 11pm and would get off at 7am. Clock in, clock out, go home, sleep, live life like an owl, no time for family or friends and repeat. Breaking away from that lifestyle was one of the hardest things I've done lately because I was so used to that lifestyle and it was secure. As hard as it was to leave I knew it was harder to stay and leaving has been one of my most rewarding experiences because so many other doors have been opened for me.

Maybe you need a job change too. You don't have to stick with the same job in order to fund your dreams. What's the harm in switching if you know you're not meant to be at any job for the rest of your life? God could have such huge plans for your life that working a job is just temporary. Just like magnets draw objects to them, mediocrity will keep pulling and tugging you, trying to keep you from accomplishing great things with your life. Mediocrity can take many forms. Negative family, friends and co-workers, or maybe your own body. No doubt you work hard all day and just want to come home and relax in front of the television while eating dinner. The next thing you know, it becomes a habit. A week goes by, then a month, then a year. You end up looking back on all the time you've wasted and it becomes frustrating because you're not any closer to accomplishing your goals. In addition, these non-productive habits have become even harder to break because you have been doing them for so long. I struggle with the same thing, friend! It just takes little decisions every day to break that magnetic tug. Consistency is hard to establish and maintain but are you willing to take the right steps forward today in order to live the life you really want?

Day 51

Equally Yoked

2 Corinthians 6:14
Be ye not unequally yoked together with unbelievers:
for what fellowship hath righteousness with unrighteousness?
and what communion hath light with darkness?

Honestly, I used to despise this verse and this subject because it used to get drilled into me often. I viewed it as just another rule of Christianity that I had to follow. I was a new Christian at this time and it probably didn't help that I had a lot of rules forced on me that I didn't understand. It also probably didn't help that I knew nothing about Christianity and so I believed everything I did wrong was likely to make God angry and punish me. I'm not even kidding. I had such a wrong view of God but that's a whole other topic for another day. Anyway, I totally understand the whole "Christianity has so many rules" mindset a lot of people probably have. Yeah, it seems overwhelming and like you're not "allowed to have fun." I used to think the same way because yeah, there's the 10 commandments and you were probably taught a lot of things you should or should not do. You would rather make your own decisions and do what you want and what you think is best. I understand that too.

I don't think badly of anyone who thinks this way. What I have actually learned over time is that there really aren't any "rules" for Christianity. Rules usually get enforced. If you speed too much over the limit, you get a ticket. There are plenty of examples I could use to illustrate the role that the law plays to ensure that we abide by those regulations. On the other hand, God doesn't force anyone to do anything. What we usually view as "rules" are more like guidelines because God cares about us and wants to keep us safe. Furthermore, God will not punish you if you choose not to follow His guidelines. I'm gonna get real with you now, so I hope you're ready because this may sting a bit. Let's say you're unhappy with some situations in your life right now. Well, whose fault is that? Not God's! Why are people so quick to blame God for bad things when we were making our own decisions, weren't we? So, you've made some mistakes. So have I and so has everyone else. All we can do is learn from them and move forward so we don't have to keep making the same mistakes. In the future we can choose to follow God's guidelines so we can have more favorable outcomes. We can certainly avoid some mistakes or trouble and personally, I'm all about avoiding pain and even things that waste my time.

I've come to embrace many of God's guidelines and by default I have chosen to uphold certain standards for my life. By having these standards I don't feel deprived in any way. I actually feel more fulfilled. I even have more respect for myself. Anyway, back to our verse. When it comes to dating and our search for our significant other, I have realized that if someone didn't have similar standards or values as me, then I would be wasting time with that person. When the Bible talks about being yoked, I think of a team of horses. You wouldn't want to yoke up some horses with some camels if you plan on getting somewhere. It just wouldn't make sense. Horses are built for strength and speed. Camels are built for a slow, steady pace. That would be a perfect example of being unequally yoked. For me, I don't consider starting a relationship with anyone unless I know they're a Christian. Have I always upheld that standard? Nope, and I got hurt. That was my bad, not gonna let that happen again. Obviously, I have other standards and guidelines because I want to eliminate as many time wasters and possibilities of getting hurt again. I sincerely want to avoid being yoked up with someone who isn't going in the same direction as me, or even someone who isn't going at the same pace as I am. Sure, someone could be a Christian, but do they have dreams and goals or do they settle for average? If they're average, how likely are they to support and encourage you to chase your dreams or goals? Just as righteousness and unrighteousness, or darkness and light are such polar opposites that they can't coexist with each other, it wouldn't make sense to be teamed up with a partner who is essentially bad for you. I probably just offended somebody. Probably because the truth hurts. I can't say anything I haven't personally experienced, so I honestly say all this out of love. Friend, are you tired of the results you get from your decisions? How about choosing to follow some of God's guidelines for your life so you can have better outcomes in the future?

DAY 52

Your Life Is A Story

Matthew 5:21
His lord said unto him, Well done, thou good and faithful servant:
thou hast been faithful over a few things, I will make thee ruler
over many things: enter thou into the joy of thy lord.

One of the reasons I love music so much is because I enjoy taking the time to listen to the lyrics. Even as a young kid, the lyrics would form a story in my mind and my imagination could play a movie in my mind. Since I love writing it doesn't surprise me that even as a kid I viewed songs as 3 minute short stories with a beat and a catchy tune.

One thing that occurred to me as I got older was that my life and everyone else's lives were also stories. We are not the authors of our lives because we can't control everything that comes our way. God is the author of our lives. He allows certain things to happen in order to test us and help us overcome obstacles so we can become better than we are now. Movies are basically books in action. There is a storyline, a plot, main characters who overcome incredible odds. Our lives are all different and made up of different hardships. A vast majority of who we are has been shaped by what we have faced and overcome. We didn't choose how our stories began and there are probably some circumstances we wish we wouldn't have had to face, but we can choose how the middle and end of our story plays out. I don't mean how you die because nobody is in complete control of that. What I mean is, you can have your life exactly the way you want it. If you have a dream to be a nurse, you should do whatever it takes to make that a reality. Is there somewhere you have always wanted to live? You should make arrangements to move there! Even if it's little you deserve it!

Since you're not dead, your story isn't over. It doesn't matter how old you are. Even if you're 90 years old, the best chapters of your life are still being written. I have a wild imagination. Sometimes I often wonder, if I had been alive during the time when the Bible was written, what would the story of my life be like? Would I have even been mentioned at all? Would my life be like one of the heroines such as Ruth who was smart enough to recognize that there was nothing left for her in her hometown so she decided to leave her old life behind and follow her mother in law to start a new life? Would I have been brave like Esther to stand before my husband who was also a king to petition on behalf of an entire race, risking my life and reputation? I always hope my story would be about having great faith to overcome many obstacles with help from God. I wish I could say in my story that I never doubted God or feared what He was doing with my life, but I'm not perfect. I don't have unshakeable faith. I do hope that I can be known for having a big heart, helping others, being sensitive to what God wants for my life, and having the courage to follow my dreams that God put in my heart. I hope that I can accomplish what God has in store for me before my time is up.

I am blessed to be alive during the era I am a part of. I am thankful because I know God doesn't make mistakes otherwise I would have been born at a different time. I know I am alive now so that I can influence many people's lives within the time frame God has given me. I know the same is true for you too! You are alive during the exact time frame that you were meant to be because your story is unique. You are meant to impact certain people with your life that I can't. So, I want to throw out a challenge to you. Maybe currently, you don't know how you want your story to end. I'm challenging you to figure it out and then start living in a way that will get you to your happy ending. Think about people from the Bible who encourage you or even people in today's world that inspire you. Sometimes I even use negative motivation. If you don't know how you want your life to be, then start with how you don't want it to be and work from there. I think about Samson a lot. I believe he could have accomplished many more great things with his life if he hadn't allowed himself to get involved with Delilah. Samson's story started out great! He was chosen by God and blessed with incredible strength. He performed amazing tasks! But his story ended as a broken and blind man who died while taking his enemies to the grave with him. Personally, I believe it was never God's intention for Samson to die with his enemies, but for Samson to have victory over them. Friend, how is your story going to end? Will it end in victory or defeat? Fear or faith? Joy or sadness? It's up to you!

DAY 53

Money

1 Timothy 6:10
For the love of money is the root of all evil: which while some coveted after, they have erred from the faith, and pierced themselves through with many sorrows.

I am actually super passionate about the subject of money. I think part of it is because I grew up hearing the phrase "money is the root of all evil." I think I first remember hearing that in a social studies class. My teacher at the time, made that statement and then backed it up with several examples from history where people had been killed over money. I don't really remember much else from that lesson other than being completely sold on that opinion. Another reason why that belief solidified itself in my mind was because of the church groups I was exposed to. I was taught to believe that if you cared a lot about money and nice things, then you were labeled as "materialistic" and you weren't "spiritual enough." *Gag* I was young, a young Christian, therefore easily influenced because what did I know? It took me quite some time to reverse this wrong mindset. It started with when I realized the phrase, "Money is the root of all evil," was actually a Bible verse taken out of context! Isn't it just like the devil to manipulate scripture in order to brainwash society in a certain way so that he can have control over them?

So, let me clear this up for you. Money is not the root of all evil. The love of money is the root of all evil. When you love money over everything else, that's where you will mess up. I'm pretty sure I've said it somewhere before but money is a tool. It can be used by good people to do good things. It can also be used by bad people to do bad things. I just want to see more money getting into the hands of the right people. Isn't it funny how most of the time the people who say money is evil are judging others who are a step above where they wish they could be? Maybe that person honestly worked hard and deserves that income, and the judgmental person would change their tune if they suddenly won the lottery. In other words, they won't put in the time and effort to earn a significant income but they sure wish somebody would give them a handout. I said handout not hand up. There's nothing wrong with getting a hand up or help when you need it. At some point or other we will all be in need of help from someone. That's a part of life because troubles will hit us all. I'm independent for the most part and I hate asking for help but God has been working on me in this area lately because I have had to ask for a lot of help recently. These times of hardship usually last longer than we want but in retrospect, they are always temporary.

I'm probably going to step on some toes, but, to me, people who go around looking for handouts and never contribute back to society are perfect examples of lazy and selfish individuals. Furthermore, I hope they stay broke unless they can learn to be open minded and stop judging others because of their success or wealth. People like this are also perfect examples of what average looks like. Average people don't want other people to succeed. I believe it's mostly because they're too much of a coward or lazy to create their own success so they have to put others down and try to keep them at the same level. Bottom line is, why would the Bible be full of verses promising blessings to us if money was evil? God loves us and wants us to be blessed beyond our wildest dreams. It's up to you to chase down your dreams and goals and God will back you up. Only you can walk your journey with God. If you're not happy with where you're at, you can fix it!

Day 54

Walking By Faith

2 Corinthians 5:7
For we walk by faith, not by sight:

'll be the first to admit that walking by faith is one of the hardest and scariest things to do. As humans, we usually want to know that everything is going to be ok before taking on things that involve a risk. Some of my scariest moments have taken place during road trips. I love traveling. Road trips are a blast but when my car starts doing funky stuff, I get a little nervous.

I remember one time I was about 5 hours into the trip and my car overheated. I had to pull over to put antifreeze in it. A nice guy pulled over to look under the hood. He couldn't see anything majorly wrong and he showed me the way to the nearest gas station so I could buy more antifreeze. Well, I was halfway. I could go back home and not risk my car anymore, or I could keep going. I decided that the devil was messing with my car, trying to scare me so that I would go back home. I chose to keep going because I believed there wasn't anything seriously wrong with my car. So, I finished my trip while making frequent stops every couple of hours to put in more antifreeze. I wouldn't trade that experience for anything. My faith in God grew tremendously. Also, my car was able to be fixed for an affordable price, so nothing major.

I also remember another time that I was running low on gas and I was on a stretch of the interstate where there was nothing but farmland on either side of me. I had already been on this stretch for a while and I was getting nervous because it looked like I would still be for a while. I couldn't even remember the last time I saw a sign for a gas station. Finally, tired of the negative dialogue in my head I blurted out to myself, "What are you worried about? You're not going to run out of gas. Within the next 5 miles there's going to be a gas station because God isn't going to let you run out of gas or be stranded. He's not going to let anything bad happen!" So, I started counting down the miles….1….2….3…. By now I was getting nervous again. Negative thoughts kept creeping back up and I fought to push them back away. I kid you not, by mile 4 I saw a sign signaling that a gas station was coming up! Words can't express how relieved I was! I wouldn't trade that experience either. I don't know about you but I get a bit of a thrill when I'm in a situation where I know I need God and He has to come through for me because by me placing all my faith in Him I can feel myself being stretched to new limits. When I'm in those situations and God does come through it does wonders for my soul.

What are you going through right now that scares you a little bit? Whatever it is, I believe the devil is trying to get you to doubt God. God will always come through for you if you can muster up the faith to believe it. Think about all the times God has come through for you before. He's not going to start letting you down now!

F.E.A.R
False Evidence Appearing Real

Psalm 23:4

Yea, though I walk through the valley of the shadow of death, I will fear no evil: for thou art with me; thy rod and thy staff they comfort me.

I love acronyms! Especially this acronym for fear! I think about this all the time when I'm being challenged in my faith. Trusting God is scary when we don't understand what's going on or why something is happening. When I'm tempted to give in to my fear and doubt God, I just remind myself that it's false evidence appearing real. When I'm worried about how my bills are going to get paid, false evidence appearing real. God has always met all my needs before and He isn't going to stop now. When I'm outside in the dark and the wind shuffles the leaves in the trees just right and a twig snaps and my mind screams "zombies!" I know it is definitely false evidence appearing real... and too many horror movies!

So, maybe you heard someone say something hurtful about you. They are just judgmental or jealous and don't know all the facts. That's false evidence appearing real. Maybe you have been fighting for years to make one of your dreams a reality. Just because they haven't come true yet doesn't mean they never will! That's false evidence appearing real! Maybe you are allowing yourself to think negative thoughts about yourself. That is definitely false evidence appearing real! Those thoughts are absolutely not true!

What lies rooted in false evidence that appears to be real have you been believing? What has been keeping you from taking action and living in victory?

It's Ok To Not Understand

Isaiah 55:9
*For as the heavens are higher than the earth, so are my ways higher
than your ways, and my thoughts than your thoughts.*

When I was a new Christian, I really struggled to understand this verse. I have a bad habit of being hard on myself on a regular basis but especially when I make mistakes. This verse was like another reminder of how awesome God is and how much I wasn't in comparison. The thing I've actually learned lately is that God isn't trying to brag about Himself and make us feel bad about ourselves. I think that what God is trying to tell us is that He always has a bigger plan for us. So, whenever you go through something difficult and it's hard to understand why it might be happening, there's probably a good reason why. I really get it. It's not always easy to have this perspective when life gets hard. Maybe you have been dealing with something for a while and you can't see a light at the end of the tunnel, let alone believe that there's a reason for your struggle. In the midst of hard times it's even more difficult to believe that something miraculous is about to happen in your life. God is preparing you and me for something amazing! It definitely is hard when you don't know how long you're going to be in this rough period.

I know God and I aren't on the same time schedule. I want things to fall into place as soon as possible. Like yesterday, or two weeks ago!

Right now, I'm in what feels like the longest waiting game. God closed a door recently in my life and I'm 100% sure He is opening a new one for me. It's just that so far I'm on day 22 of knocking on this door and whether or not it opens all the way is to be determined. I've been trying to figure out if I will be ok if this opportunity slams shut in my face when truthfully it's something I have wanted ever since I was a kid. To finally come this close to obtaining it and imagine having it jerked away from me would be devastating. Up until this point I have fully believed this is the direction God has been leading me, and yet, I can't help but wonder if I have been wrong and wasted all this time. I'm sharing this because I hope it helps someone as much as it is helping me. As much as I really desire for this opportunity to work out, I think I will be ok if it doesn't. You better believe I will be disappointed. You better believe I'll probably cry and even be angry for a little while. When that's all said and done, emotionally, I'll pick myself back up again and I'll be ok. I'll remind myself that I've made it through harder situations than this and I'll know God is still going to take care of me.

I have to trust that He has a bigger and better plan for me otherwise none of it would matter. God is working on me so that I can be a better Christian and a better individual in general. He is working on you too. Sometimes I think maybe if we knew when something difficult was coming we would choose to opt out. If we opt out of the difficult times we couldn't grow in the process. We wouldn't become who we are meant to be all along nor could we reap the other benefits associated with the victory of our tribulations. Storms don't last forever! This too shall pass. Hang in there. I believe in you!

Day 57

I'm Down But I'm Not Out!

2 Corinthians 4:8-9
*We are troubled on every side, yet not distressed;
we are perplexed, but not in despair; persecuted, but not forsaken;
cast down, but not destroyed;*

Well, I got some disappointing news this morning. A dream I had since I was a kid of working for a particular company fell through. It looked like it might finally be a reality because I was so close to obtaining it! I was so sure God was going to finally open this door of opportunity for me and I was ready to go barreling through it. I pictured myself wearing the uniform and how happy I was about to be. Go ahead and laugh but I wanted this job for about 13 years which is exactly half my life. I don't know why it stuck with me all these years but I just thought it was cool and I never knew how to achieve my goal because I always thought you needed to know the right people in order to get on there, or had to have some sort of experience or fill in the blank that I didn't have. Not to mention I have tried a few times before now to get on and hadn't had any luck. Once when I was 20 and lived in North Carolina, once around last December 2018 and this year in May 2019.

This last time looked so promising. I finally got a call from them! To make a long story short, over the course of the past 22 days, I had two interviews, waited about a week for the local hospital to schedule me in for a physical, drug test and agility test. One week I went to the plant 3 days in a row. Two of those days were just to try and talk to someone who could get me connected with the right person for an interview. By the way it took about all the faith and courage I had to drive all that way those days because it's about a 45 min drive each way and I had no idea if I could get an interview at all. The rest of the 22 days were pretty much waiting. Waiting in between the interviews, waiting for the hospital to get me in, waiting on results from my tests, etc. I figured I already waited 13 years I could keep waiting now that I was closer than ever before.

Then, the phone call came this morning. I didn't score high enough on the agility test. Basically a computer says I'm not strong enough… grrrr! I want to bust up that computer and see if it still thinks I'm not strong enough! Besides feeling a little angry and disappointed, I'm really ok with the result. I mean, don't get me wrong, I have cried off and on all day but I gave this my best shot because it was what I wanted. Yeah, it feels like I wasted a lot of time and I still fell flat on my face. (Pretty hard fall too!) However, there was a time in my life when I didn't have the confidence to go after what I wanted. I didn't used to take risks or fight for myself. I would just stay in a miserable position. So, even though I failed, I still didn't lose completely. I'm still growing and changing. This won't be the last time I fail at anything and at the end of the day, I'm ok. God has taken care of all my needs and He will continue to do so. Yeah, so one of my dreams didn't come true, but one doesn't have an "n" in front of it. Meaning just because one dream doesn't happen, it doesn't mean "none" of my dreams will come true. Yeah, I'm a little bit down, but during one of my down times today, I was thinking about how even as bad as this rejection hurts, I'm still not ready to give up on other dreams.

Maybe you have been in a similar situation where it looked like things were finally going to fall into place for you and then suddenly the rug gets jerked right out from under you. It's so hard to comprehend and as much as you want to quit on everything, you need to realize that God is still here to catch you. I love the end of today's verse where it talks about being cast down, but not destroyed. That describes exactly how I feel today. It doesn't matter how down I feel, I know I'm never going to be destroyed because the enemy doesn't have that kind of power over me! He doesn't have that kind of power over you either!

DAY 58

Scars Tell Stories

1 Peter 2:24
Who his own self bare our sins in his own body on the tree,
that we, being dead to sins, should live unto righteousness:
by whose stripes ye were healed.

You guys, I'm a tomboy, so, I'm covered in scars! Most of them are from my childhood. I played outside, climbed trees and wrecked my bike a lot! I'm a walking accident waiting to happen. I'm so clumsy I can fall up and down the stairs. As a kid, I played hard because I thought I was invincible. Today, I know I'm not. I've had several stitches and broke a finger once. My point is I remember the story behind them. I'm reminded whenever I see them. I'm kind of weird actually because I'm sort of proud of some of my scars. I had one scar that was my favorite. It has kind of faded but I'm pretty sure it's still there. Anyway, I got it from my high school softball days.

One day at practice the infield was covered in mud because it had rained so much. I think a lot of the girls were actually surprised that practice hadn't been cancelled. I was but I got over my surprise pretty quickly and just went with it. I remember thinking, "Ok, we're gonna do this. No problem." At the end of practice we had to slide into the home plate before we could go home. That was the muddiest spot on the whole field. When my turn came, there was mud scooped out around the plate from where the other girls had went before me. For whatever reason, I chose to slide in on my stomach with my left arm out in front of me. My arm hit and slid so hard across the edge of the plate that it cut about an inch and a half slice in my arm. Let's just say that cleaning that out in the shower later wasn't exactly fun. I literally peeled the skin off like you would peel the skin off an apple or a banana. The skin flopped around as I examined it (a little grossed out) all bloody and muddy. I loved the scar it left though because it reminded me of being covered head to toe in mud and how fun that was!

Not all scars are fun though. I highly doubt, and I believe I'm correct in my assumption that when Jesus looks at His scars He doesn't think, "Oh, yeah, these scars are from the nails in my wrists when I was nailed to the cross. That was fun!" I also don't think Jesus enjoyed getting whipped and beaten right before His crucifixion. However, I am willing to bet that when He sees His scars He is proud because He can say, "I got these the day I bought back the human race and defeated Satan once and for all." Nobody else who had or who will ever live can say that. Jesus will forever be proud of that because He loves us enough that He was willing to die for us. Don't feel unworthy. You are totally worth every scar Jesus earned that day!

DAY 59

God is Full of Surprises

Psalm 34:10
The young lions do lack, and suffer hunger:
but they that seek the Lord shall not want any good thing.

k! So, this morning God surprised me again! Remember how I shared about failing my agility test that I needed to pass in order to get hired at the job I was really wanting? Well, I thought that was the end of the road for me and I started looking somewhere else for employment. This morning, May 23, 2019 I got another call from my preferred job for another position! Even though my score on the agility test was too low for the original position I wanted, it was high enough for this other position. I was absolutely blown away! Yesterday I was trying my best to stay positive but I was still full of disappointment. I was going to start researching companies that I can get an insurance plan with since I was about to age out of my mom's insurance. As a type 1 diabetic I knew I really needed to make sure I was going to be covered. After believing it wasn't going to work out, I saw my last hope of securing health insurance fly out the window.

To put things into perspective for you, one year in January when our insurance deductible hadn't been met, I had to pay close to $1,000 just to get my two types of insulin I needed. One type usually lasts two months, the other type lasts about three months. Normally whenever I get refills, between the insulin and various other diabetic supplies, (needles, alcohol swabs, blood glucose test strips, and lancets) I usually spend $200 every two to three months until the deductible is met. I really couldn't afford the price on these items without any insurance. Not to mention I was thinking about dental and vision coverage I would need.

After the good news today, I was so surprised, amazed and incredibly thankful! I honestly believe this is a blessing from God and a reward for my faith in Him to take care of me. Sure, it has been a roller coaster of emotions for me the past couple of days and sometimes I wish that wasn't a necessary part of my walk with Christ, but I do have to admit how thankful I am for all the growth I have experienced! My faith in God is at an all time high! I wish I could say that I knew God had something else planned the entire time, but there were a few moments where I doubted Him, or at least I doubted myself in that I thought I knew where He was leading me and then thought perhaps I had misunderstood Him.

It's incredibly difficult to experience having a dream snatched away from you, but also having a hope for a really good insurance coverage when you depend on it so much. Obviously, today, I feel so silly for doubting Him even though I was at peace with the situation. (Before I knew I was still getting a position.) This is why I say God is full of surprises. Today's verse is a perfect reminder for me how truly blessed I am! God is pointing out how animals in the wild sometimes go hungry because their lives are hard. I'm sure your life has been hard at times too just as mine has. No matter how hard it gets though, God is promising He will take care of all our needs. He certainly did for me! He gave me a position with an exceptional company, a company I have wanted to work for since the age of 12, and He solved my need for insurance coverage! God is not a respector of persons. He doesn't favor me more than you. I'm sharing this with you because I hope it encourages you to believe that God will come through for you just like He did for me.

DAY 60

America Is Still God's Country

Matthew 18:20
*For where two or three are gathered together in name,
there am I in the midst of them.*

If you're like me, maybe sometimes you get discouraged or worried about the direction our country is going. I won't be presumptuous and pretend I have any idea about the exact turning point that tipped the scales in the wrong favor. All I know is that we are living in the days that Proverbs 21:2 talks about where "Every way of a man is right in his own eyes." Too many people are so quick to betray others as long as it is profitable to them. In their mind it is ok. In today's world, somebody else is always getting offended and seeking revenge. They feel justified in trying to destroy somebody's life just because they said something they didn't agree with. On another note, religious freedom is encouraged and defended almost every time with the exception of Christianity. Christians are attacked and face persecution. The world and America is slowly turning away from God. People don't want to hear that their decisions or lifestyles are wrong. They don't want to hear the truth. Probably because the truth hurts and is uncomfortable. Too many people operate under the assumption that they can only be friends with those who have the same opinions and values. It really doesn't have to be that way. If I cut out all the people in my life who had different views than me, my life would be very lonely.

I think for sure that Christians are seriously outnumbered by unbelievers. That could be why the country is rapidly plunging. Our voice no longer truly matters. Those that are in leadership positions are trying to please the masses whose voices are louder than ours. It is hard watching such a great country be destroyed from within. It is such a slow process that most people can't recognize that it is even happening. I refuse to watch the news because it only causes more strife and division. It is hard to stay optimistic in such troubling times, but as with other hardships in my life, I have an even harder time with completely losing hope. There have been so many times where I felt like permanently giving up. I probably would have been justified in doing so and at times I have given up. However, in the end God has always gotten me through. If He cares enough about me to help me through all my troubles, then I have reason to believe that He is taking care of all His other children and collectively, our nation. As bad as things continue to get, I just can't bring myself to worry about it for too long because I know as a result everything will be ok. Things will keep getting worse, but God will be with us to make sure we come out safely. With the right perspective, nothing seems so bad once you know that one day when you finally meet God and live with Him in Heaven, you will realize that none of what is happening now will even matter anymore. Until that day comes, I still choose to believe that America is still God's country. I can definitely count more than three Christians that I know. If that is true, then I believe that God is still here working in our lives and protecting us.

In Genesis 18:16-33 Abraham pleads with the Lord not to destroy an entire city because there are righteous people who live there as well as the unrighteous. Abraham was able to talk God down from sparing the city for the sake of 50 righteous people down to 10! Meaning if they just found 10 people who lived their lives in a way that was pleasing to God, He would not destroy the city! I can still name way more than 10 people in America who are Christians trying to do their best to serve God. If that's the case, then how could such a loving, compassionate God ever abandon us? Especially if we come together and continue to pray for our country. It is now more important than ever before that we stand together united and not divided. Together we can accomplish more. Together God will hear us.

DAY 61

Is That How I make You Feel, Lord?

Hebrews 4:15 a
*For we have not an high priest which cannot be touched
with the feeling of our infirmities;*

I can't stop thinking about you. I miss you. My heart is longing for you. Things were so wonderful. What happened? How long must I wait for your heart to turn back to me? Will your heart turn back to me? How can you push away someone who loves you? All I feel is sadness and hurt.

Is that how I make you feel, Lord?

I'm still confused at how abruptly things ended. We used to talk every day and now it has been months since you cut me off. Should I give up waiting for you to come back? Is there a chance that you will? I just feel so confused.

Is that how I make you feel, Lord?

I miss the sound of your voice. I miss your laughter. I miss those carefree days when you wanted to spend time with me. I miss your presence. Now I just feel empty.

Is that how I make you feel, Lord?

Whenever my mind gets jumbled and my emotions feel like they're going to burst out of me, I like to write so I can get them out. Writing is probably my best form of therapy for me. Then, occasionally, when I'm in the decompressing stage of writing, I get hit with great ideas. I wrote the above passage a few years ago when I was going through a breakup. I had only been with the guy for three months but it was the longest relationship I had been in and I was just crushed when he ended things. I have always had a big heart and cared for people on a deeper level than is probably normal. As a result, a lot of people have come into my life and left. When they leave I don't forget them. I still wish them the best and don't have any ill will towards them. I do wonder how it was so easy for them to leave though. There have been people who I thought I would be friends with for the rest of my life, but now we haven't spoken in years because of their pride. So, I just continue doing my best and move forward anyway without them.

In the midst of me feeling sorry for myself, and trying to figure out the "why's, or the "what I could have done differently's" was when I was hit with the thought, "Is that how I make you feel, Lord?" Then I thought of all the times I have gotten backslid in my relationship with God. It's during these times in my life that I unintentionally pushed God away and stopped speaking to Him. It was as if I was breaking up with God because I have left Him behind. The longer I go without including Him in my life, there becomes a seemingly overwhelming chasm between us. It becomes awkward each time to go back to Him. It is the same with other broken relationships. Maybe they get permanently broken or maybe they can be fixed. Depending on the situation and who it is, all hopes of a healthy relationship might not be lost. Possibly a relative has let you down and caused discord. If it is really important for you to have that bridge gapped, perhaps they feel the same way and will work with you to resolve the issues. Some relationships, you will come to find out, you are better off without. It isn't always easy to know at first which ones you should let go of and which ones you should keep working on. Hopefully God helps you differentiate between the two as He has done for me throughout the years. Also, it is my biggest hope that you can always find your way back to God as I always do. He is never the one who abandons us. He just patiently waits for us to come back to Him every time.

DAY 62

I Guess I'm One of Those "Jesus Freaks"

Psalm 62:7
*In God is my salvation and my glory:
the rock of my strength, and my refuge, is in God.*

Testimony: A public recounting of a religious conversion or experience. (Definition from the Oxford Language Dictionary)

The other day I happened to be thinking of my testimony. I used to be in a position where I had to tell it to the public all the time. As a teenager in my late teens, I was enrolled in an all girls Christian Academy. I graduated from there and spent about a year and a half enrolled there. The older man who owned and operated the school was an evangelist so we travelled all the time. More Sundays than I can count, we would be attending a different church where he would preach. These churches would take up an offering for him and the academy. Before he would preach, he liked for all of us girls and the dorm mom to stand on stage and quote scripture and sing. He would even ask a few of us girls to tell our testimony. I was one of them more often than not. I got over my fear of public speaking pretty quickly but it's still not my most favorite thing to do. Anyway, it led me to think about how different my testimony would be today if I shared it. In many ways I'm still the same but in a lot of ways I couldn't be more different. I received salvation when I was 16 years old. At that point, my life already looked very different from most people my age or even twice my age. I didn't grow up in a religious home but I believed in God. The older I became, I got more angry and bitter and I began to believe in God less. I began to reject anything that had to do with God or religion. I rationalized that if God existed, then He was to blame for all the bad things that had happened in my life. If He loved me then why did He continue to let bad things happen?

Fast forward to the day I received salvation. I was angry at the whole world. It was a Saturday and I had already spent two days in the county jailhouse. Yep, you read that right. That is a long story in itself. The circumstances that landed me in that position should've never happened and wouldn't have happened if I had been in the care of a competent adult. But, I wasn't so on a Saturday morning I was invited to attend a "church" meeting. I only accepted so I could stretch my legs and have an interaction with somebody. I was also slightly curious about what this lady had to say and why she was visiting inmates. A small part of me knew she had to know something I didn't because obviously I was doing something wrong. I wanted answers but I didn't want to hear about how God loves me. I heard that before but I felt like He had abandoned me. In addition to that, I felt like He rejected me and hated me. She certainly told me something I had never heard before. She told me the message of salvation and why I needed it. In that moment nothing else mattered. She asked me, "If I died right now, did I know that I would go to Heaven?" I told her,"No." Two years previously I attempted taking my own life. I thought if I was successful and met God, I hoped He would understand and forgive me. I thought He would allow me to live in Heaven because Hell was for "bad" people who murdered others or who committed a lifetime of unspeakable acts. I was only 14. I hadn't committed any crimes that bad. But I didn't know for sure what would happen to me when I died and I didn't know that you could know for sure that Heaven would be your final destination. I just figured that you could earn your way to Heaven or that you would just have to find out when the day came and hope for the best.

Long story short, before that lady left that day, with tears streaming down my face and feeling like the dirtiest criminal in the history of the world, I accepted Christ as my Savior. I felt like the weight of the world was lifted off my shoulders. I felt so light I thought it was amazing that I actually wasn't floating up into the air. That was in 2010. I've never been the same. I've been through some difficult times even as a Christian and I wouldn't have been able to make it without God's help. I've strayed from Him too many times to count but I'm not perfect. I do feel miserable when I have caused division between myself and God. I feel guilty when I go long periods of time without talking to Him or attending church. Basically, I know God is real and our relationship is real. He truly completes me. I know He speaks to me and calls me back to Him when I'm straying. I literally feel the tugging on my heart to come back to Him. Eventually, I always do find my way back to Him because He never gives up on me. This is my updated testimony. The fact that I can attest to God's faithfulness, patience, mercy, forgiveness, and love because I have witnessed it on multiple occasions in my life. No matter how long or hard the road in life gets, God has always been there every step of the way.

Before I was saved, I used to make fun of Christians because I didn't understand. How could you have a relationship with someone you have never met? I used to call people like that a "Jesus freak." They were weird and probably a little bit crazy. Now the tables have turned. I figure if I like going to church, listening to Christian music, reading faith based Christian books, reading the Bible and I love Jesus because He first loved me, then I must be a Jesus freak too. I am perfectly ok with that!

Day 63

What An Awesome Heritage

Psalm 16:6
*The lines have fallen onto me in pleasant places; yea,
I have a goodly heritage.*

If you're like me, and probably a majority of you are, when it comes to a heritage or an inheritance, you won't be left with acres and acres of land or millions of dollars. That's ok. Wealth can come in many forms. After my grandma moved and changed her address to Heaven, I discovered some pretty neat things. Now in my possession is my grandma's Bible, her mother's Bible and her grandmother's Bible! To me, I'm super proud to have them in my safekeeping. It tells me that I come from a line of excellent Christian women! I count myself extremely blessed to be their descendent. Even though I never knew my great grandma or my great, great grandma, I feel a sort of emotional connection to them. They helped pave the way for me. I literally wouldn't be here if it wasn't for them. I definitely feel a sort of respect for them. I can't wait to meet them in Heaven one day when my time on earth is over. This is pure speculation but perhaps in Heaven, God operates much the same way with the residents there that He does with us who are still on the earth. I'd like to believe that my ancestors run to God on my behalf and ask Him for His protection over me. And because they were so faithful with their lives, God listens to them and answers their requests.

I think even on our worst days we are all incredibly blessed. At the end of the day, no matter what has come our way, we are still blessed. In the end, I'm not too concerned with what will or won't be left for me monetarily or otherwise. When I'm in Heaven none of it will even matter anyway. I'm trying to stay focused on the day when I do get to Heaven. With God as my father, I stand to gain a much better inheritance that will last me for eternity. We are all promised mansions to live in. There won't be any bills or taxes to pay. There won't be any dirt or dust to clean. No more pain, sickness or suffering. Heaven is supposed to be so beautiful we couldn't even begin to fathom, describe or understand. Gates of pearl, streets made of gold…yes, please! I'd rather inherit that! In the meantime, my plan is to keep fighting the good fight and carrying the legacy my grandma and ancestors left me. I feel a sense of responsibility to finish what they started and to finish well!

DAY 64

Where's the Instruction Book for Life?

Psalm 119:105
Thy word is a lamp unto my feet and a light unto my path.

As a teenager, I remember starting to figure out that the choices I make would have a huge impact. Should I go to college vs. not go to college? Where should I go to college? What should my major be? Did I have good enough grades? What was I interested in? What should I commit to for the rest of my life? What scholarships should I apply for? I had no idea what I wanted my life to look like or how to make it happen. I wished there was an instruction book to tell me which steps to take first. I've come to learn in recent years that you can't get anywhere without a destination first. If you don't know what results you want, you can't form a map or instructions to help you get there. It starts with you and your desires. Before you can go any further, you have to figure that out. How do you expect God to give you the desires of your heart when you don't know what you desire?

After becoming a Christian, I soon learned that the Bible was the instruction book for life that I needed! So, in your instruction manual for your life, the first step is to figure out what you want. Where do you want to end up? It might seem sort of odd but you do have to sort of work backwards. With your end goal figured out, you can determine little by little what the next step above that might be and so on and so forth until you get to the beginning where you are currently at. Then, you can follow the steps in order to get where you want to. It won't always go perfectly as you planned, but it's better than nothing and I'm confident that God will show you which steps need to be added or taken out along the way. As long as you trust Him, He will be with you the entire way to make sure you don't get lost and that you reach your destination. There have been periods of my life that I knew what I wanted to do but I had no idea how to accomplish them. Those were hard, frustrating times but I just kept doing what I already was while I waited on God to show me how to get to the next step and what the next step was. Maybe you know what the next step is but you're missing a link in getting to the next step. You literally can't move because you need help from God. There could be a hundred different factors that come into play and you're feeling confused or anxious wondering how God is going to come through? Maybe you're excited to find out what God has up His sleeve to surprise you with next! I think that God intended it to be that way. He likes when we depend on Him. It helps build our faith. We do everything we can in our power, then, when we can't go any further, we keep praying, reading our Bible, (our instruction book) for more clues, keeping busy with what we know we should be, waiting and trusting God, and then when the time is right God leads you to your next step. Then the cycle starts again.

I think the Bible is more than a list of "do's" and "don'ts." If I had never picked up and read the Bible, I don't think I would have the faith to believe that God loves me and wants me to succeed more than I want me to succeed. I wouldn't even have the desire to know God better or even believe that my wildest dreams can and will come true! Through scripture, I have conceived my own personal instruction book for my life. I believe it is possible for you to do the same thing. I'm not saying the Bible will tell you where to go to college or what profession you should choose, but the more you read the Bible, it will become ingrained in you. The more familiar you are with it you will be able to have better judgment when it comes to making major decisions. Follow the option that gives you the most peace. Little by little, things will start falling into place for you. It is truly an amazing experience. It is also a very intimate experience. The journey is between you and God. My journey thus far has been very exciting and fulfilling! I hope that everyone reading this gets to experience God in the same ways I have!

DAY 65

God the Gardener

Psalm 1:3
And he shall be like a tree planted by the rivers of water,
that bringeth forth his fruit in his season; his leaf also shall not wither;
and whatsoever he doeth shall prosper.

I'm not going to lie. I'm not a huge fan of gardening. Don't get me wrong, nothing tastes better than fruit and vegetables grown from a fresh garden than bought in a store. I also love admiring flowers that have been kept in immaculate condition. In other words, I like enjoying the fruits of someone else's labor. Gardening takes a lot of work! Sometimes the ground is hard, weeds continuously pop up, you have to make sure bugs and animals don't eat up all your crops. The work is endless. You really have to dedicate a lot of time to stay up on top of the work so the garden stays healthy. Not only that, but you would want your garden to produce as much as possible. It would be hard for your garden to flourish and yield an abundance if the plants were being eaten or not getting enough water. Their growth would get stunted. I always thought it was neat how much could grow from one tiny seed. As long as it is taken care of, it will bloom and multiply itself just like God intended it to.

I like to think of myself as a tiny seed. Well, maybe spiritually I've grown some, but God is definitely the gardener. He's been working on me for a while. He's cultivating me into something beautiful, strong, and amazing. I can picture God pulling out weeds in our minds, and watering our hearts. He wants us to grow in Him. The more we walk with Him, the more He will reveal about Himself to us. Imagine growing and flourishing so much that there will be no area in your life that will be lacking. "His leaf also shall not wither; and whatsoever he doeth shall prosper." I don't know about you but I could use a little prosperity in my life. Maybe you want to start your own business or change jobs. Maybe you want to move to the location of your dreams. Do you feel called for something greater, but you have been too afraid to pursue it? Whatever it is, I think it's time to take the plunge and go after it. Even if it's something that's smaller that will bring some sort of degree of happiness to your life. We were made to prosper and with God helping us, how could we not be prosperous in everything we do? Maybe it will just take a little bit of time, but why not get started and learn to enjoy the journey along the way? Why not learn to enjoy the process of growing?

When Are You Going to Stop Hating Yourself?

Romans 3:23
For all have sinned, and come short of the glory of God.

When I first became a Christian, one of the hardest things for me to understand was how God judged all sin the same way. I always thought someone who committed murder was way worse than stealing for example. I also used to think that there were "levels" of sin that were worse than others. Maybe we think this way in order to not feel as guilty about our own sins. However, whether you have told a lie, or had mean thoughts about someone, God sees it all the same way. The devil will use any excuse to keep you from becoming close to God. First the devil tells you your sins are not as bad as those that other people commit so you don't need God. Then, he will try to tell you that you can't ever be perfect so you may as well not even try because you're going to sin every day. Before you know it, guilt sets in and takes up residence in your life. Yes, I'm speaking from experience. Unfortunately, I have spent a lot of time living in guilt. Sometimes, no matter how hard I try, I lose patience with someone and get angry. Or I get burnt out and don't perform my best at work. Or I even hold grudges against someone. Maybe, while you're reading this, some of your faults and shortcomings are coming to your mind. For me, knowing that every day I'm going to fall short , and my past mistakes creeping up and reminding me of the things I've done easily discourage me and hinder my relationship with God.

I know He knows all my failures and I know He will forgive me, but more often than not, I get this overwhelming sense of unworthiness that completely drowns me. As a result, I have gone long periods of time without even talking to God. Then, the longer I go without talking to Him, more guilt piles itself on me along with more feelings of unworthiness. It's very easy to find yourself buried and getting back out becomes harder. For years I have struggled with this. I can go periods of time where I've grown so much and my relationship with God is the best it has ever been. Then a little while later I can't remember the last time I felt evidence of God in my life. Probably mainly because I've been beating myself up over my past. I know I can't change things and maybe that's a small part of why I spend a lot of mental energy in the past. I wish that I could change some things and it seems unfair because some things were out of my control to begin with.

Maybe you have some things you would change in your past. It's hard for us to see ourselves the way God does. God is ready to forgive us so easily, but we struggle with forgiving ourselves. It's easy to think that if things were different, maybe we would have more faith or be better Christians. However, I have to remind myself that this is also a lie designed to keep me from going to God. Everything happens the way it was meant to. I can either accept the past and learn from it or keep letting it drag me down. It was during a time that I was dwelling on the past and feeling unworthy that I heard God speak to the depths of my heart and He just asked me, "When are you going to stop hating yourself?" Then He gently reminded me that He loved me enough to die for me. It was then that I realized in a way that I was hating myself. Why should I keep hating myself when God doesn't hate me? I keep dwelling on my faults when God doesn't. I'm learning to be easier on myself. It is taking a lot of work, but it is helping. Do you sometimes hate yourself? Why? Why not come forward to God and find out as I am, exactly how much God loves you!

Day 67

I Don't Know Much!

Psalm 147:5
Great is our Lord, and of great power: his understanding is infinite.

"To infinity and beyond!" Oh, my bad! When I think about infinity or the word "infinite" I hear Buzz Lightyear's voice in my mind! Infinity is a difficult concept to grasp. It is never ending. You could say that God's knowledge is never ending and beyond that. That's a huge difference when, in comparison, there is quite a lot that I don't know. I don't just mean mathematics or rocket science. I mean the reasons behind the difficulties life throws at us. The real and the hard things. I don't know why babies have to fight hard for their lives, spending a majority of their lives in hospitals while their families look on helplessly before their bodies give up. I don't know why some people have to be in the wrong place at the wrong time and end up being victims of a homicide. I don't know why so many people are killed in automobile accidents but the drunk individual behind the wheel of the other vehicle gets to walk away without a single injury. I don't know why women who desperately want to start a family have to battle infertility while other women who take their children for granted can get pregnant so easily. I don't know why dogs have to get run over. I don't know why grandma's have to leave us way too soon. With all the evil there already is in the world, I don't know why there has to be cancer and a multitude of various other sicknesses and diseases.

In the book <u>The Hiding Place,</u> the author Corrie Ten Boom, who was a Holocaust survivor, tells a story that has always stuck with me. She recounts a time where she asked her father a difficult question. They were about to get off a train and her father asked her to carry his suitcase. Upon discovering and admitting that it was too heavy for her, her father used the situation as an analogy to her question. He told her, "It would be a pretty poor father who would ask his little girl to carry such a load. It's the same way with knowledge. Some knowledge is too heavy for children. When you are older and stronger, you can bear it. For now you must trust me to carry it for you." I believe the answers to all our difficult questions in life are probably like a heavy suitcase. I think as hard as it is to not know all the "why's" it would be harder to walk around with all the additional baggage. It would slow us down, trip us up, and wear us out. This is why God carries our "suitcases" for us. He loves us too much to add to our load. He carries it because He is helping us. While God's mind and knowledge is infinite, ours is finite. Our minds are limited. Maybe God knows that if we did have all the answers to the tough questions, we may still not be able to fully understand.

One day when we join God in Heaven, I believe He will reveal all things to us because only then will we be more like Him. We will have all our limitations removed. For now, I'm content with letting my heavenly Father carry my suitcases. I can trust Him enough to know that He isn't keeping something good from me, but rather He is helping me with something that is difficult and could potentially cause me more unnecessary hurt or additional struggles.

DAY 68

A Delay Is Not A Denial

Read Daniel 10:12-13

*I*f you read a few verses above Daniel 10:12 you will understand that Daniel was visited by an angel. This angel basically tells Daniel that he heard Daniel's prayer on the first day that Daniel began praying. In addition, the angel reveals that he was on his way to deliver Daniel's answer on that first day but that he was detained for 21 days by the enemy. Sometimes we assume that God is withholding answers because it takes a long time for an answer to arrive. This may not always be the case. Yes, God always answers in His perfect timing, but what if your answer is literally on its way right now and is just being detained? With this mindset, it encourages me to not entirely give up. What if you do give up praying and then your angel only gets detained even longer? I'm learning this concept recently because I have a few requests I've laid out to God over the last several years and I've gotten discouraged and given up at times. Maybe you can relate too. I'm not the most patient person. I'm working on it, but when I pray, I want God to answer immediately. Also, I have a confession. Sometimes I get lazy with my prayers. I don't know how much of it boils down to faith or laziness or some other reason, but a lot of the time I don't even pray for things because I know that God knows what I'm thinking and He can provide an answer before I even ask. While this is true, and it has worked in some instances, God has been showing me more and more lately how crucial it is to just be disciplined enough to take the extra step and go ahead and ask Him anyway. Ask Him even though He already knows what you're going to say. Ask Him even though you have already asked Him several times before. Ask Him even when it feels like He's not listening. Ask Him even when you're tired of asking. I'm beginning to understand that this is just how prayer is supposed to work effectively.

Usually the thoughts that I have that don't turn into a prayer before God answers them, are not even anything major. They're just a little taste to keep building my faith. It's like God is saying to me, "I've provided this small thing just to prove to you that I care. I'm paying attention to even the minor things without you even asking. Now imagine the things I would do for you if you asked. Imagine the things we could do together." What if when we pray, we are actually helping our angels? What if they need reinforcements and our prayers give them the strength they need to keep fighting the enemy in order to deliver our blessings we have been faithfully asking for? If you're struggling in your prayer life, I encourage you to get a copy of Mark Batterson's book, The Circle Maker. Every time I read it my faith grows tremendously and I'm encouraged to keep praying for things again that I had previously given up on. What prayers have you given up on? What if tomorrow is the day your answer comes, will you still give up today?

DAY 69

Be Thankful For Unanswered Prayer

John 14:27

Peace I leave with you, my peace I give unto you: not as the world giveth, give I unto you. Let not your heart be troubled, neither let it be afraid.

Garth Brooks said it best in his song "Unanswered Prayers." Garth sings these lyrics in the chorus, "Sometimes I thank God for unanswered prayers. Remember when you're talkin' to the man upstairs that just because He doesn't answer, doesn't mean that He don't care. Some of God's greatest gifts are unanswered prayers."

I used to get so confused by this song and these lyrics because I used to think that every prayer that went unanswered was an opportunity that I was missing out on. I believed that my current reality at the time was God's second best for my life. Isn't it so easy to think that we know what's best for us? After all, it's our life. We know what we want better than God. Now give yourself a face palm! Seriously, I want to shake my head and roll my eyes at those statements. That's how I know I've come a long way from where I used to be spiritually. They always say hindsight is 20/20. That is so true! We as humans are so fickle! What we want one day can change the next day. We can't see the future. We can barely think long term. A lot of people don't think past the next Friday night. God knows the future. He knows how it would negatively affect our lives if He gave us everything we asked for. God's motives are literally to protect us, so how could the path He is leading us on be second best? It's hard to see right now, but He is leading us down the best path for each of us. Our path isn't supposed to look like someone else's.

Maybe you feel like your life is standing still or that you're being passed by everyone else. I keep finding more and more each day that I actually am thankful I didn't get what I thought I wanted. I used to think I wanted to be married and have children by this point in my life. Looking back, I think I only wanted that because everyone I knew wanted that. I actually enjoy the freedom from the responsibility of raising children. I also honestly believe if I never get married, I'll be just fine. I have such a strong, independent streak that I have a hard time imagining some-body else in the picture helping me with anything because I'm too used to handling things on my own. I'm thankful God has kept me from a lot of unnecessary heartache. I think a part of maturing spiritually is being able to be at peace with where you are in your life. It's crazy in the best way possible how that peace only God can give you actually feels. I honestly don't know how to describe how wonderful it feels. Do you know the peace I'm talking about? Do you have areas in your life that you are unhappy about because God said, "No," to some of your prayers?

It's difficult to make the transition from believing God should give us this prayer or that one, to accepting what God wants for us. It can almost feel like God is pulling us in the opposite direction from what we want. In reality, He is trying to gently lead us down the path meant for us and we are trying to pull God with us toward the direction we want Him to go. I really just think that what it all boils down to, is we just have to quit pulling God. Just let Him lead and find the strength to somehow have faith in Him and trust Him. Once we are able to do that, it opens the door to peace and an unlimited amount of possibil-ities. You might even discover that where God is leading you, is actu-ally where you wanted to go all along. Your way probably just looked more promising but could've ended up in a dead end or even have been pretty dangerous. It's kind of funny how eventually God's desires and your desires can end up lining up perfectly.

DAY 70

I Want to Be Like Noah,
But I'm Actually More Like Jonah

Hebrews 11:7
By faith Noah, being warned of God of things not seen as yet,
moved with fear, prepared an ark to the saving of his house;
by the which he condemned the world, and became heir
of the righteousness which is by faith.

I'm sure if you take a moment you could name a handful of people from the Bible who lived amazing lives because they had the faith to trust God and they served Him faithfully their entire lives. God used these individuals to accomplish some of the most incredible miracles of all time. On the other hand, I'm sure you could think of a few people in the Bible who did not make very wise decisions who helped bring about the destruction of their own lives. I wish I could say I was like Noah. Noah had a lot of faith in order to build an ark and try to warn others of the impending danger of a flood. His faith didn't waver even when everyone else mocked him. Noah saved his entire family as a result of his faithfulness. Some days I feel like I have a lot of faith. Other days I have my doubts about God and His will for my life. This is why I feel like a lot of the time, I'm more like Jonah. Jonah had his own doubts about serving God. It's also likely that he was afraid of being used to accomplish great things. After all, it can be a huge responsibility. Luke 12:48 says: For unto whomsoever much is given, of him shall be much required.

In addition to being afraid, Jonah actually got on a ship and was trying to run away from God and the responsibility God was trying to give him. We all know that didn't go over well! Jonah got swallowed up by a whale and eventually ended up surrendering to God. Luckily, Jonah's story ended with a redemption arc. He didn't ruin his life and he was able to be used by God to accomplish great things. Even I have run from God over the years. I've been angry, hurt, biter, confused, and much more. In that time, I've lived my life in doubt and resentment. I let numerous excuses and distractions take over my life and keep me from fulfilling the things I know I'm meant to do with my life. Fear has even crept in and kept me hidden in the shadows. Who from the Bible is an inspiration to you? Who do you want to be like? Who do you feel like you actually relate to the most? Have you been running from God and His calling on your life? The good news is, it's never too late to stop running. Just like Jonah, you can have a redemption arc in your story. It's up to you. I've had to learn the hard way that my faults and failures don't define who I am. Your faults and failures don't define who you are! Your choices do though! What choice are you going to make today?

DAY 71

From Walking to Sinking

Read Matthew 14:28-31

*I*n this passage you read about how Jesus walks on water witnessed by the disciples. Peter was in awe and felt compelled to walk out to sea to meet Jesus. I wonder how many steps he was able to take before doubt and fear crept back into his mind and he began to sink? I have a hard time imagining the faith he must have had to begin with! I've never walked on water but I've definitely been in situations where I felt like I was following God's instructions and then shortly after, I had found myself sinking and calling out to God for help. I believe, just like Peter, I witnessed the sea of my life become unsteady from boisterous winds which caused my faith to waver.

When Peter decided to take that first step on the water, he made a HUGE decision! Huge decisions are always scary in the first place. Peter knew that he was safe in the boat. He was risking his own safety by stepping out of the boat and surrounding himself with nothing but water. Along with giving up his safety, Peter was leaving his comfort behind. He was leaving the known for the unknown. Maybe there's a certain circumstance that comes to your mind in your life. Maybe you're in a situation right now and you feel like you're going to sink. Maybe you can hear God calling you to greater things but you're too scared to leave the comfort of your current reality. Whatever the case may be, rest assured knowing that you're not going to sink! Peter cried

174

out to Jesus and was rescued. If you have been following God, He is going to take care of you! Let the waves and winds of life come at you. They can't hurt you. Keep your eyes focused on what you know you need to do and you will always be taken care of. God is always going to lead you to something better for you!

Almost 3 years ago, I was in one of the most uncertain stages of my life. I had been working a 3rd shift job for way too long. I had become absolutely miserable. I believed God could provide me with a dayshift job somewhere else. I waited several months before finding the "perfect" opportunity. 6 weeks after working at the new job I was suddenly laid off. I was shocked! I thought this was where God was leading me. What had once been an open door that opened so easily suddenly slammed shut! I was a little bit angry and later nervous. I had never been laid off or fired from any job before. I was usually the one to leave jobs on my own terms. I began to question my choice to leave that 3rd shift job that I knew was a little too secure… I wondered if I should go back? Did I misread God's leading? I tried not to worry too much. I had some money in a savings account and my grandparents let me earn some money working for them. A lot of the time I went over to my mom's house for dinner and for other meals I ate a lot of ramen noodles.

I had a couple of promising looking job opportunities at this time. One that I knew would be a 2nd shift job and one that I felt I had a good chance of getting a spot on 1st shift. Plus, the 1st shift job was for a company that I really wanted to work for. All together I spent another 6 weeks of being unemployed. And don't get me started on how the government failed me during this time! Even though I had always been a hard working citizen, contributing to society, paying my taxes etc the place of employment that laid me off disputed my attempt to collect unemployment! I was furious! My savings account became depleted. I sold my couch to keep making ends meet and I was facing the possibility of missing my next house payment. I was even considering finding temporary homes for my 3 dogs because I wasn't sure if I could afford food for them. Those 6 weeks really tried my faith! But they also built my faith and I grew really close to God. I could've taken either of those night shift jobs but I felt like I would lose the dayshift opportunity forever. I had to find a way to keep sticking it out. I just knew that was what I wanted and I couldn't settle for less. I knew God was going to come through because He had already led me through multiple doors with this company. I was just waiting to make it through the final door. To make a long story short, God came through and I got the dayshift job! My first paycheck hit the bank the same day my next bill was due! Whew! That was a little too close for my liking, but God has literally never failed me! In the past 2 ½ years of working at this job, God has helped me to pay off two credit cards, over three thousand dollars of medical debt, I've purchased the vehicle of my dreams, (a 2015 maroon F150 which had been a dream of mine for about 7 years) and I also added another dog to my family! God totally led me to where I am today! He didn't let me sink. If He can perform these miracles for me, I know He can come through for you!

DAY 72

God and Dogs

Genesis 2:19

And out of the ground the Lord God formed every beast of the field, and every fowl of the air; and brought them to Adam to see what he would call them: and whatsoever Adam called every living creature, that was the name thereof.

I have always been fascinated with the whole story of creation. It all started with the first man and woman that God created. God entrusted the earth and all its inhabitants to Adam and Eve. Throughout the years, generation by generation, the safekeeping of the earth has been handed down. Now, in 2021, things are a little crazy. I don't contribute much as far as taking care of the earth, but I own four awesome dogs! Dogs can be a handful but I made a commitment to them once I brought them home. My dogs have taught me so much. They can be so much fun in addition to companionship. Not to mention, just plain cute! Dogs really are special in their own way. I love how "dog" is God spelled backward. There had to be a reason that they were given that name. Which leads me to all my dogs have taught me about how they are similar to God in many other ways.

1) They are the true embodiment of unconditional love! Whether it has been five minutes or five hours, my dogs are always excited

to see me. Nothing beats the welcoming I receive every time I come home from a long, hard day at work.

2) Dogs make amazing friends. They love to spend time with you. Whether it's a lazy day at home or a road trip my dogs are always ready! If I suggest we should go to bed, my dogs will all run into the bedroom. If I say, "Do you guys want to go for a ride?" I can't get them out of the door fast enough!

3) My dogs absolutely love going on walks. I don't know what the appeal is but it's one of their favorite things to do! I figured it was a neat correlation because we walk our dogs and we also refer to our spiritual lives as a walk with God.

4) Just like God is a great listener, dogs are also good at listening. Sometimes I just like to talk to my dogs even though I know they don't understand what I'm saying. The main reason I do this is because it is amusing to watch them sit perfectly still and look at me while I'm talking. I really love it when they tilt their heads from side to side as if what I'm saying is really interesting, or as if they're trying really hard to understand me!

5) Dogs are extremely loyal. They won't betray you. They love you too much. In fact, some breeds, ingrained in their personalities is actually the motive to protect you at all costs. Unfortunately none of my dogs are guard dogs but some will attack if they feel threatened or if they believe their humans are potentially in danger. Evidence of God's protection is all over my life!

6) Lastly, when you are upset, they want to comfort you. There have been numerous times where I have cried and it visibly upset my dogs. In their own way, they have tried to comfort me. They have laid down beside me or nudged me or climbed in my lap. I believe God is upset when we're hurting too because He is our father. No parent likes to see their child cry. Do you have any dogs? In what ways have I missed that you think dogs are like God? I hope you give your dogs an extra special hug and take the time to spoil them a little bit!

DAY 73

Be Thankful For Things You Don't Normally Think About

1 Thessalonians 5:18
*In everything give thanks:
for this is the will of God in Christ Jesus concerning you.*

We live in a busy world. We spend a large portion of our time working and then with the time we have left over, we are catching up on chores, taking care of children, taking care of pets, squeezing in time with family or friends, trying to find time to relax and maintain a decent sleep schedule. We get so rushed to try to get everything done. We have so many expectations crammed into our day. When you're busy it's easy to become stressed and hard to be thankful. I wouldn't be surprised if this was all the devil's design. If we're kept busy and distracted all day, by the end of each day we're so tired we can't wait to crash and hit the sheets. The busier we are, the less likely we will be to make time for God. We know we should pray and thank God for a new day but we are already running late for work. We know we should pray over our meal but we have to rush the kids to a ball game, so drive thru for dinner it is. Your job has been requiring you to work six days a week so you're only left with one day to enjoy or get caught up on housework? It's hard to feel thankful when you're exhausted and spiritually burned out. When I get up for work at 3:30 in the morning it's hard to feel anything besides grumpy as I try to figure out what to make for breakfast.

Lately, I have been thinking about how I have a lot to be thankful for. This mainly started because I have been making myself make time for God. I have been making myself pray. In addition, I have been making time for other things. I make time to walk my dogs. They enjoy it and I know the exercise is good for me. I make time to focus on my goals and a roadmap for how I can accomplish them. When you focus on your blessings it really helps put your mind in a better state. When your mind is positive, your emotions will follow suit. I have been in a mode of thanking God lately for His blessings. Then, it occurred to me that I should try to thank God for things that I don't normally think about. When you take the time to think about all the not so obvious things that we usually take for granted, it opens our eyes to how ungrateful we can actually be. I challenged myself to list as many things to be thankful for that I could for 20 minutes. I came up with a list of 70 items. The last few minutes were a struggle. My mind went blank. Somehow we have so much to be thankful for that we should be able to literally continue thanking God without end, but our minds aren't even capable of understanding and comprehending everything that God does for us.

The devil doesn't like for us to have an attitude of gratitude. He would much rather have control over our minds and have us be stressed and depressed. He knows if we're thankful, we will draw closer to God. When was the last time you made time to thank God for your blessings? How many things can you list to be thankful for in 20 minutes? What items are on your list that are not immediately obvious to you?

DAY 74

Stop Worrying

Matthew 6:34

Take therefore no thought for the morrow: for the morrow shall take thought for the things of itself. Sufficient unto the day is the evil thereof.

I would definitely classify myself in my early adult years as a worrier. I think a lot of that stemmed from the fact that I felt completely unprepared for "the real world". I faced a lot of opposition and I had a lot to figure out. At 18 with no real work experience nobody wanted to hire me. Other places required a college education. Again, I was 18-19 so how was I supposed to already have a college degree? It was a catch 22! Super frustrating! I moved around a lot and lived with different friends and my dad at one point trying different locations hoping that something would give and I could land a decent job. It wasn't until I felt like I had nowhere else to turn that I decided to leave my life in North Carolina behind and try to build a new life in Iowa with my mom's help. This was right before I turned 21 and I can honestly say things have been so much different. For a while I even worked two jobs at a time just to stay busy and save money while trying to meet some goals.

On most jobs I really wanted, I haven't been denied. I earn way more than I could've ever hoped to while living in the south. Anyway, little by little, over the years, I think this confidence has flowed over into other areas of my life. The journey has been long and hard but

I can definitely tell that God has been taking care of me the whole time. When you go from earning $800 a month and constantly worrying about how you're going to make it through each month, to now owning my own house, driving the vehicle of my dreams, earning 3x's the amount I was as a young adult, and having a small amount in savings, and getting to enjoy the fruits of your labor, it does become hard to not be thankful. It is hard for me to worry about pretty much anything when all my needs and more are being met. Of course, I'm always going to want more. I'm human, my flesh is weak and it seeks to fill my life with fun, flashy objects. It is a struggle to not always give in, but I'm finding a nice balance.

As far as worrying goes, I have become the complete opposite of the way I used to be. I make it a practice to turn things over to God that are out of my control. Another hard battle has been my health. I can't control the fact that I became a type 1 diabetic at the age of 23. I don't understand the reasons behind the circumstances, but God spared my life for a reason and so I figure as long as He decides to keep me here on this earth, I will try to keep being faithful and serving Him.

I really don't like a lot of the things that are going on in the world, but just as I can't control my health, I recognize that I have no control over the government or the current pandemic. I don't want to belittle the circumstances, but I'm just not going to live my life in a constant state of fear. If I get a sore throat or the sniffles, I'm not going to jump to the worst conclusion and worry myself that I might need to quarantine. I believe if I did catch the coronavirus then God would take care of me every step of the way. If that day ever comes, but I choose to keep living my life free from worry.

On the topic of worry, there are a few points that I believe are worth mentioning. First and foremost, God plainly tells us not to worry. My life became way more simple when I learned to relinquish control of my life over to God. It isn't always easy but it has been more rewarding. It has lifted unnecessary stress from my shoulders and from my mind. Have you ever noticed how much worrying actually affects your health?

I'm not an expert and I haven't done any research, but I know from my personal experiences. I used to get frequent headaches and feel down. Now, my headaches are few and far between. I've also experienced more really good days because I've been able to focus on that present day and enjoy it rather than constantly worrying about the next two weeks or the next month. In other words, worrying too much can steal your joy. I don't think it's a bad thing to have plans or be prepared for the future, but to a point you need to be flexible because not all plans are going to work out exactly the way you want them to. You can't let factors outside your control allow you to get bent out of shape.

Ultimately the biggest takeaway is that I've witnessed God work too many times for me to worry. It actually takes more effort for me to worry now than to let go of situations and let God handle them. He just continually amazes me with all the things He does and how He provides. One thing I do struggle with is being patient with people who are worriers! I either get frustrated or have to fight the urge not to laugh. The things that people will allow to get under their skin is mind blowing. I want to say, "You really waste mental energy thinking about that?!" I just can't fathom worrying about something that may never come to pass. I challenge you to start letting go of worrying and start trusting God more. It won't be easy at first, but it is so worth the peace at the end of the day!

DAY 75

Mom Upside Down Is Wow

Read Corinthians 13: 4-7

This passage is about love. God is love. The next best thing that comes to mind where love is concerned, are all the mothers in the world! It can't be a coincidence that the word "mom" also spells "wow" if you flip the "m's" upside down. This thought crossed my mind the other day as I drove home from work. I have a 45 minute commute so my mind tends to wander. Anyway, I happened to be thinking mainly about my mom and "wow" kept coming to the forefront of my mind. Besides me, my mom has three other kids. All four of us have presented our own share of difficulties while growing up. Somehow three of us have reached adulthood and we still manage to get along (mostly) even though there are age gaps. Amazingly, my mom still looks young too! All jokes aside, she's one of the strongest women I know and I know I wouldn't want to face some of the things she has went through. It takes incredible strength, love, selflessness, patience, commitment, courage, responsibility, and wisdom to be a mother. Becoming a mother isn't just being a provider for the next 18 years of your child's life. It's a journey that you embark on together. Each growing and learning from the other. Both must accept neither party is perfect, but also try to enjoy the journey along the way.

As I get older I find that I view my mom as a companion more than anything else. Sometimes I don't exactly need anything, but I feel the urge to call her and hear her voice. I have a lot of friends that are mothers and I respect them tremendously. They are shaping the future generations to become mature, responsible human beings. That is no easy task. Also, I'm amazed by how fierce their love for their children can be. There's a reason for the nickname "mama bear!" Just as I wouldn't want to be on the wrong end of a mama bear's fury as she protects the lives of her cubs, I pity the soul of those who dare to come between some of my friends and their children in any way!

This goes without saying, but is still worth the mention. Moms are also amazing because of their ability to create, carry and nurture their offspring. The ability to carry a growing baby and give birth can take a huge toll on the mother but I believe the reward makes up for the hard work. At least that's what most of my friends will tell you! That experience is exclusive to the mom, forming a bond between herself and the unborn baby. What memories come to your mind when you think about your mom? When was the last time you called her up just to hear her voice, or to tell her how much you appreciate her?

DAY 76

There's Nothing Wrong With Wanting To Give Up

Luke 22:42
*Saying, Father, if thou be willing, remove this cup from me:
nevertheless not my will, but thine, be done*

It's been another day. Life is tough. Maybe you are just hoping whatever struggle you're going through will hurry up and get over with. You've probably thought something like this, "Why this?" or, "Haven't I been through enough?" or "I don't know how I'm going to get through this."

I have no idea what you're facing and there's a good chance that even if I did know, I'm sure I wouldn't be able to relate to how you're feeling. I do know that how you're feeling is perfectly normal. Your feelings are real and you deserve to feel them and take your time to work through them in a healthy manner. Only you can determine what that might look like to you. I also know that when things get hard and continue to be hard, it can become extremely easy to be overwhelmed and want to give up. There's nothing wrong with wanting to give up either. Don't allow yourself to feel guilty or think that you're weak for feeling that way. You're not a bad Christian and you don't lack faith. You are being human. Accept that you're not perfect. In Luke 22:42 Jesus is actually praying to God and asking to be let off the hook. He knew His death was drawing near and as much as He knew He needed to follow through, He was also scared. Jesus was as much human as He was God.

Sometimes I'm guilty of forgetting that every feeling I've ever experienced, Jesus has too. Having this perspective makes it a little bit easier to keep carrying on. The devil would want you to feel discouraged and make you think that nobody understands your struggles. As long as he can make you believe that you are alone, he can keep more control over you. Obviously, he wants to keep you down so that you are not a threat to him. Falling down and getting discouraged are a natural part of everyone's spiritual journey. As hard as the struggles may be, I believe the times when you fall flat on your face and feel hopeless are very important to our spiritual growth. It is then that we are usually left with no choice but to reach out to God more desperately. We become more willing to place our faith in Him (unfortunately if you're like me) because we may have exhausted all our other avenues to accomplish an end to our obstacles. I wish I could say I always turn to God first thing when troubles hit, but being the stubborn, independent woman that I am, I tend to try to figure things out on my own first. Eventually, I will turn to God every time. Even though I know in the end I'm going to go to Him, I have been guilty of going to Him as a last resort. However, the victory in this is at least I'm learning to bring my struggles to God much quicker than usual! In the times that I'm down, I learn more about myself, work on myself to be better, and learn more about God. Then, before long, just like every other time, I regain my strength and get back up.

Every time life brings us to our knees we get the opportunity to rebuild ourselves. It seems backwards to accept that if we keep falling apart, rebuilding and growing again it will actually make us stronger and better than before, but it is absolutely true. God wouldn't want us to remain the same any more than He would allow us to fall apart and rebuild just to go through the pain to become what we were when we fell apart. It is during this process of coming undone and rebuilding that we are able to decide which parts of our lives we need to abandon and which parts to keep or adopt new ones to rebuild with. When you're starting over, it's always best to take a good look at your foundation and make it stronger than ever. For me, my foundation is my relationship with God. Usually, I notice my life begins to crumble when my relationship with God is weak. Once I repair that, I'm able to get rid of hurtful habits and replace them with better ones. One last thought is that as many times as I have felt like giving up completely, I never do. It's not to brag on myself, because I am extremely weak. I'm bragging on God because even though I may give up temporarily, God always helps me get back up and keep going. He loves me and you too much to leave us lying on the ground surrounded by the rubble of our former selves. God continuously reminds me that as long as I am still here on this earth, I don't have the option to give up because He is always going to be here to help me. Even if He has to carry me, He's not going to leave me behind. He lets me stay on the ground for a while, but then He comes along and lets me know it's time to get up.

Are there situations in your life like this that come to your mind? If you're currently on the floor spiritually, are you ready to get back up and rebuild? Do you feel God's presence urging you to stand up and follow Him again?

Day 77

Stop Defending Yourself

Deuteronomy 32:35
*To me belongeth vengeance and recompence; their foot shall slide
in due time: for the day of their calamity is at hand,
and the things that shall come upon them make haste.*

This verse is one of my favorites when it comes to handling my enemies. I think it would be unrealistic to believe that you are going to make it through this life without making any enemies. Even if the strife is completely one sided and you don't harbor any ill will toward anyone, at some point I'm sure someone has or will have hard feelings toward you. None of us are perfect. We will get taken advantage of, gossiped about, or bullied, etc. When we are mistreated it is so easy to hold a grudge. It is even natural to want to seek revenge. It goes against the grain to take a step back, lift up your hands and turn the situation over to God. Before I go any further, let me explain. This is not another one of those lectures to love your enemies! Yes, God does say we should love our enemies, but maybe, like me, you have some enemies you can't imagine yourself ever loving. I said it. I'm nowhere near the best Christian I should be. So I content myself with the knowledge that I stand somewhere in between loving and hating my enemies. I honestly don't believe I hate any of my enemies either. I know hating is wrong and God views hatred the same as wishing harm or death on your enemies. Since I know how it feels to be wronged, I don't want to cause harm to anyone else including the handful of individuals I don't particularly like. In all reality, the best I can do concerning my enemies is pray Deuteronomy 32:35 over their lives.

I'm not yet in the place spiritually where I can pray favor and blessings over them, but I am a huge believer in reaping what you sow. Over the years I have seen God avenge me in some areas over enemies from the past. I think that has made it easier to relinquish control in more recent struggles. No matter what your enemies or mine have done, sooner or later they will get what's coming to them. I firmly believe that God can allow much worse destruction to hit their lives than anything we could do in retaliation. Besides the obvious potential trouble we could attract on ourselves by retaliating, isn't it worth considering the relief of knowing you don't have to handle the situation? To put it another way, isn't it better to ease your own mind of the stress of worrying about how you're going to "get even" by washing your hands of them and watching God come to your defense? You literally don't have to defend yourself! Honestly, I think the best part of all of it is that when God does come to your defense and destroys your enemies, you are completely blameless! There's no way it can be traced back to you and potentially cause any backlash! Out of pure speculation, God had to have known how difficult it would be for some of us to love our enemies. That is why I think this verse exists. That way it will hopefully open our eyes and motivate us to want to trust God. The Bible is full of stories of God allowing victory over one's own enemies. Just as surely as God delivered the enemies into the hands of His children in times past, He will do the same for you and me. Hopefully this verse will help you like it has helped me tremendously! Are you ready to pray Deuteronomy 32:35 over your enemies and watch God work?

DAY 78

Learning the Hard Way

Exodus 12:31
And he called for Moses and Aaron by night, and said, Rise up,
and get you forth from among my people, both ye and
the children of Israel; and go, serve the Lord, as ye have said.

To be perfectly honest, reading the handful of chapters where Moses continually tries to persuade the Pharaoh of Egypt to release the Israelites from slavery is really unpleasant. Previously, I didn't really mind reading those passages because they are a part of the Bible and they are interesting. However, it used to be way too easy for me to throw shade at the Pharaoh and judge him. I would think, "If I was him, I'd have let the Israelites go from the beginning and save my people all the trouble and heartache that was bound to follow if I don't." Clearly he was warned multiple times and he kept hardening his heart. He kept refusing even though destruction would hit afterwards each time! It was only after the Pharaoh's oldest child and all the other Egyptian's first born children were tragically slain that he finally allowed the Israelites to be free from bondage. His permission, at this point, came way too late! Up until that point, any other opportunity to give in would have been more ideal. Instead, he chose to pay the ultimate price. How could he have been so willing to put his own child's life at stake in addition to so many other innocent children?

I have a hard time accepting that the Pharaoh could have been a fair or competent ruler based on his poor decisions. If I had been under his rule and lost a child, I would be furious with him and want him to be overthrown from his position. Eventually, the Pharaoh did realize the error of his ways but he learned way too late and he learned the hard way. I think this is why I can admit that I sort of relate to the Pharaoh as I get older. I definitely have had to learn some things the hard way. Thankfully, none of my consequences have been as devastating, but I have caused myself heartache and stress that could have been avoided. I would be lying if I said there weren't times when I kind of felt God warning me not to make some choices but I did it anyway. I can say, it is very humbling to come to God and admit you were wrong and He was right! Maybe you can relate. Since none of us can go back in time to undo our mistakes, the best thing we can do is try to do better moving forward. After you ask God for forgiveness, be sure to forgive yourself. Then learn from your mistakes and try not to repeat them. The hard truth of the matter is since not one of us is perfect, the only way we learn anything is by making mistakes.

I hope you are better at forgiving yourself than I am. I struggle with this concept but I'm making progress every day toward getting better at it. I know God is willing and able to forgive all my mistakes and forget them, therefore, so should I. I have to constantly remind myself that God thought so much of me that He died for me. Since this is true, every time I refuse to forgive myself, I am minimizing the sacrifice Jesus made on the cross. To put it another way, Jesus' blood He shed is stronger than any sin I could or have committed. Especially because His blood is powerful enough to cover every sin ever committed. So when I deny myself forgiveness, I am acting as if Jesus' blood wasn't enough to atone for my mistakes. We should never seriously dwell on this concept because deep in our souls we know that this isn't true. We know that God forgives us, so we should too. I know, easier said than done. Hopefully if you struggle like I do, God will help you to get better at forgiving yourself like He is helping me.

Don't Be Scared of God

1 John 4:16&18
And we have known and believed the love that God hath to us. God is love; and he that dwelleth in love dwelleth in God, and God in him.

There is no fear in love; but perfect love casteth out fear: because fear hath torment. He that feareth is not made perfect in love.

As a young Christian, new to Christianity, I was easily influenced in the ways of God. I figured I had a lot to learn and so I did try to learn a lot. However, my problem was that I was in a position where a lot of rules and beliefs were forced on me. I was in a girl's academy full time and so I had to uphold the strict beliefs held by the staff. They controlled every aspect of my life for about a year and a half. Don't get me wrong, it wasn't all bad. I met some amazing people that are still a part of my life today and who had a huge impact on me becoming who I am today.

My biggest complaint would be the fact that not only was so much forced on me to the point that I couldn't process anything on my own, but also throughout this period of time, I adopted an unhealthy view of God. Instead of wanting to learn more about how to have a relationship with God, I became more reluctant because I had begun to be afraid of God. I was being taught that so many things were "wrong" or "bad" and that God could choose to punish me if I did this or that. I honestly don't know how much I prayed during that time frame because I felt too apprehensive to even try to approach God. I was constantly waiting for the shoe to drop. It's kind of hard to get too excited about serving God when you're scared of Him!

It would have been more beneficial to focus on teaching us about God's love, grace, forgiveness, patience, or understanding. I've had to spend the last several years discovering exactly what standards are actually appropriate for me and my life. Thankfully, my relationship with God has improved tremendously because nobody is forcing anything on me. I have been able to take the time and space I needed to experience one on one time with God. Funny enough, God has taught me so much more because He used love. Whenever I was skeptical if I should approach Him with my small concerns, He showed me how He even cares for the sparrows that fall. Whenever I feel too ashamed to ask Him for forgiveness for the same thing for about the hundredth time, He showed me He removes our transgressions as far away as the east is from the west. When things in my life are going great and I walk with an extra spring in my step, God whispers to me that He wants to bless me more abundantly. Even during the darkest storm of my life when I'm consumed by grief and pain, God told me that He would carry me. I don't think I had actually needed God to carry me before and I didn't even have the strength to refuse Him, even though I kind of wanted to. He knew my need was too great to be ignored and He did carry me through the darkest hours I have ever faced because I had no strength or desire to go any further on my own.

I have finally begun to find out what it means to know God as a Father and a friend, not just as a Lord or King to be served out of obligation. I can talk to God because I want to and I feel more at ease doing so since I'm not afraid or made to. I have embraced my role as a child of God and I haven't been apprehensive about asking Him for things. He has answered a lot of my prayers and I recognize that I am extremely blessed. It saddens me to think that other people are probably struggling with this concept. Literally, my whole spiritual life has changed because

I felt loved by God. It brought me a sense of confidence and security that I had never experienced before. I strongly encourage anyone reading this to block out all the "noise" of this world and focus on your relationship with God. If you take the time to address the areas that need improvement, it may just end up being a complete game changer. God isn't going to neglect you. He will love you through it.

Lastly, don't continue for another moment to allow the lives of others to get you off track. There's always going to be someone else who thinks that you should do things differently. The moment you bend and bow to those influences you risk jeopardizing all the progress you have made. In addition to that, you might even lose your true self. I couldn't describe all the times I used to feel like I had an identity crisis because I was living my life according to what others told me was the Christian way to be and I didn't even recognize myself anymore. Everyone's Christian walk looks differently. Just take things at your own pace. I can't stress this enough! And don't be scared of God!

The Faith of a Mustard Seed

Matthew 17:20

And Jesus said unto them, Because of your unbelief: for verily I say unto you, If ye have faith as a grain of mustard seed, ye shall say unto this mountain, Remove hence to yonder place; and it shall remove; and nothing shall be impossible unto you.

I have probably stated before that this life we all live is incredibly difficult. Everyone has their own battles they face that most others have no idea about. Some of these struggles may be big or small. The size itself is of no significance. What seems small to you might be big for someone else. Both big and small problems are worth addressing. Your problems can feel as if they are as big as a mountain. I can totally relate! It is super discouraging spiritually to look up and see an enormous mountain directly in front of you. When you close your eyes at night you see it because it is constantly on your mind. When you're awake, you feel exhausted because you can't see around it and have no earthly idea how to solve your problem and make the mountain vanish. Just thinking about getting around it or over it seems impossible.

If you are anything like me, the bigger the mountain, the smaller your faith grows. I don't know why we doubt God whenever we face something new. Just because it's a different mountain doesn't mean that God is any less able to help us and lead us safely on the other side!

He has gotten each and every one of us this far and past several other mountains. Why would He stop and forsake us now? The answer is He absolutely wouldn't!

Lately, my prayers reference the mustard seed. God has brought me through so much but I have a pretty big mountain in my path currently. For this particular mountain, I could see it coming from quite a distance so I didn't let it bother me much or discourage me. My faith was bigger from a distance. Now that it's right in front of me and blocking my path the size of it is daunting! For now, yes, I have little faith. Instead of beating myself up about it though, I'm clinging to it! I've learned from the past that it does no good to be hard on yourself for having little faith. You could play that game over and over and get nowhere or you can continue working with what you have. You could listen to the thoughts that tell you, "You've been a Christian for a while! You should have more faith by now!" or you could take God at His word and believe that with faith the size of a mustard seed, your mountains will be removed! I don't know the exact size of my faith but I know it is at least the size of a mustard seed. For now, I'll take it! I like the sound of that!

One final thought. All seeds are meant to grow just like faith is meant to grow. Even our tiny mustard seed sized faith. As God helps us over our current mountains and we win the victory, our faith should grow throughout the process and become big, strong, powerful, unwavering. Perhaps when we face new struggles we just need to use new seeds of faith. It's not as if we really doubt God. Just like each tree yields fruit of its' own kind and reproduces seeds of its' own kind, when you face financial trouble you would pick your faith from your victory over previous financial struggles. You wouldn't use faith from your forgiveness tree. Maybe faith isn't meant to be limited. Maybe our faith is meant to be likened to a whole garden of gigantic, strong, beautiful, flowering trees!

DAY 81

The Devil Talks to You

John 10:10
*The thief commeth not, but for to steal,
and to kill, and to destroy: I am come that they might have life and,
that they might have it more abundantly.*

*I*f you are a child of God, the devil is on the warpath after you. He will use any strategy he can in order to keep you from serving God and thwarting his plans. I want to draw your attention to your thoughts. Our minds are very powerful tools. It feeds off of what we choose to believe. The devil knows this. That's why he tries so hard to bombard our minds with negativity. If he can get you to believe his lies about you that he whispers to you, he can steal your joy, kill your light, and destroy your life. All those lies that tell you that you're not good enough, or that you don't deserve good things. Yeah, that's the enemy all right! When you believe these negative thoughts, your self- image can drop drastically. It can ruin your relationship with God.

For several years I listened to multiple lies. I didn't recognize where these thoughts were coming from. I had just gotten so used to them being there. I really did believe them too! It's no wonder I would drift from God so much or take a while for me to find my way back to Him for that matter. These thoughts especially tortured me whenever I was having a bad day. They would start up and play on repeat like a broken

record. Finally, one day I had enough. Something clicked in my head and I realized what was going on. I sat down and wrote every single lie I had heard the most and that were the most destructive to me. Then I made a list of positive thoughts from God that countered each lie from the enemy. I think it would be beneficial for you to do the same thing. There are people out there who have had to face horrors most of us couldn't imagine in our wildest dreams. You can bet that the devil will use that to his advantage for as long as it works to keep them in bondage. It is important to be specific and counter each lie because then the next time the enemy tries to tell you that particular lie again, you can say, "Nah, God told me this and I believe Him now more than you." I'll share a few examples of my lists. You have probably heard similar lies.
Lies From the Enemy:

1) You're ugly
2) You're insignificant
3) You're even more worthless now that you are diabetic
4) You are a mistake and should have never been born
5) You will never achieve your goals and desires
6) You don't deserve a good life
7) You will never help impact anyone's life
8) God doesn't love you

Truths From God:

1) You're beautiful
2) You're important
3) You can reach people with diabetes
4) You were created for a purpose
5) You will achieve all your hearts desires
6) You deserve the best life possible
7) You will impact millions of peoples' lives
8) I do love you-I gave my life for you

Believe me, there is more where that came from. Some of them with increasing ferocity. I'm sure you can come up with a pretty hefty list too. It might take some time to listen to God and let Him refute each lie but don't let the length of time it takes to accomplish this discourage you. I think it took me several months to finish my complete list of truths. I had several years of listening to the lies under my belt that I had to start drowning out. There's something different about seeing all of these things in your own writing. It is powerful and validating. Good luck! I'm rooting for you!

DAY 82

Investing in Yourself

Proverbs 19:2 a
Also, that the soul be without knowledge, it is not good:

There are several ways to invest. You can invest money to try and grow your assets. You can invest your time into meaningful organizations. You can invest yourself in other people. I wonder though, how many of us are actually investing in ourselves? What I mean is doing things for ourselves to better ourselves so that we can ensure that we are not running ourselves on empty. When you're empty it's hard to help others that we care about. I understand everybody's life looks a little different. I encourage you to decide what's best for you and then go do those things! For example, you might want to get a degree that will help open the right doors that lead you to the career path you want. College can be a great way to invest in yourself. What about losing a few extra pounds? Why not get a little healthier so you can be around longer for your loved ones? You could go for walks around your neighborhood or join a gym.

I believe it's worth mentioning too that we should invest in our minds. If you're struggling with something, why not find a book that can help you overcome? It just might make a huge difference in closing the gap between where you are and where you want to be. Again, not all of these suggestions may be for you. Only you know what would help keep you feeling refreshed. You could even decide to do things you have been putting off. Need new clothes? Go get them! Want a day at the spa? Go! The point is, you are worth the investment! Don't look at it as an expense, but as an investment in YOU! While you're working on making these worthy investments, you might end up learning quite a few things! That's where the knowledge part comes in. A part of this life is learning in order to grow into the person you are meant to be.

Make Up Your Mind

James 1:8
A double minded man is unstable in all his ways.

Have you ever been faced with a decision that required you to make a choice and then later you changed your mind? All of a sudden your first decision didn't seem right so you second guessed yourself. I'm definitely guilty of doing this! If I didn't see the results I wanted I would convince myself that I had made the wrong choice. Then I would beat myself up because I couldn't go back in time and re-do my decision. By the way, that kind of thinking will drive anybody crazy! Nobody is perfect, so you're not always going to make perfect choices. Cut yourself some slack! I've learned to be better at making the best possible choices I can and then just accept the results for what they are. I'm not always happy with the outcomes but if I take my time reaching a decision and I feel confident with taking the necessary action to follow through with it, then good or bad, I'm able to rationalize that I did my best at that point in time. I think if you second guess yourself too much, you will slowly start creating the habit of undermining yourself and your capabilities. When you're facing a tough decision and you constantly jump back and forth on a solution, you're not exactly confident. Your confidence becomes weakened. You start over thinking, which can be bad in some cases because you will have created imaginary scenarios and give yourself unnecessary anxiety. Before you know it, your problem solving skills will have greatly diminished.

Have you ever second guessed God? Yeah, I'm guilty of that too! One minute you feel pretty confident that God is leading you one direction and the next you might be thinking, "This can't be right." So you try to take the reins of your life back and end up making things worse! It's no fun feeling like you're not accomplishing anything when you want to. At the end of the day, it's not the end of the world. Tomorrow you get to try again to do better. You can always learn from your choices. Whether they be good or bad, right or wrong. Life is full of experiences. It's up to you how you're going to handle them.

An example from the Bible of second guessing God is when the serpent deceives Eve. God gave Adam and Eve clear instructions on what they were allowed to eat and what was forbidden. All the serpent had to do was cause reasonable doubt in Eve's mind. Eve began to question everything she believed she knew to be true. She chose to act on her doubt and now we all know the consequences of that decision.

Sometimes when I'm faced with a tough decision, even though I've spent a considerable amount of time trying to figure out the best option, it can sort of feel like spiritually I'm walking on uneven ground. It feels scary to take that next step because it can feel like a giant step and you're not going to know what happens next until you take that next step. We would much rather see what happens before we make our move. Unfortunately, life, God, and faith doesn't work that way. You might take the step and fall on your face but at least you moved. God will be there with you come what may. Make your decision and more importantly, stick with it! If you change your mind all the time, chances are you will probably make an irrational or spontaneous choice. I believe that's why God was warning us that a double minded person is unstable in all their ways.

One final thought. Have you ever taken a multiple choice test and your gut told you one thing and then later you ended up changing your answer? The crazy part is a majority of the time after you change your answer you end up getting it wrong! It would happen to me all the time in school. That's why they say to trust your gut or your first instinct. I believe we could see whatever results we are looking for if we can learn to trust our own decisions we make the first time we make them instead of wasting time and mental energy constantly doubting every move we make. The same thing can be said when it comes to trusting God with our lives. If we stop second guessing God then we can get where we want to faster than if we keep pausing and reflecting or over thinking if we are on the right path or not.

Would you rather be unstable in everything you do and not witness the success you're seeking, or would you rather make a solid decision and stand by it long enough to possibly see the results you actually want?

Day 84

Work

2 Thessalonians 3:10
For even when we were with you, that if any would not work,
neither should he eat.

We are living in very strange times. I remember a time not too long ago when it was tough to find a job. Now it seems like anywhere I go that company is hiring. People used to be desperate for jobs, but now jobs are desperate for workers. It's as if work has become a foreign concept. I don't even know where to place the blame. I've met people twice my age with half the work ethic I have. I have also met children with great work ethics.

I have seen so many people come and go at various jobs I have worked. I wouldn't believe it if I hadn't witnessed it for myself, but there really are people out there who will start a job and then quit it after ONE day! I will never understand that concept. At least have something lined up before you quit and put in a notice. I have worked at places where I was completely miserable but I somehow still stuck it out until I found something else.

I understand there are people who have medical issues that prevent them from working, but I don't understand the individuals who can work but chose not to. I would describe myself as having always been reasonably ambitious and independent. As a young adult I needed quite a bit of assistance and the length of time it was taking to accomplish my goals simultaneously were driving me crazy. I had to move back in with my mom around my 21st birthday and essentially start my life over. I moved from North Carolina to Iowa. Starting over took a lot of work and at one point I worked two jobs. It took me what felt like forever to build up credit, save some money and get my car paid down so that my odds of getting approved for a loan for a house would be better. I knew the end goal was to buy my own home. I was determined to not rent from someone. Maybe it was because I always had goals in front of me is why I was able to persevere through all the difficult times when I wanted to quit my job prematurely. All together it took me about 3 ½ years of living under my mom's roof until I was able to close on the purchase of my own home.

During that time I was also diagnosed with type 1 diabetes and ended up not being able to work for a little over a month. For someone who was used to working a lot this was weird for me. I remember trying to adjust as my blood sugars were coming down and regulating. My vision was affected and being patient with my eyesight was really hard. I didn't feel comfortable driving to run errands because I couldn't read road signs clearly and my reflexes were slower. I felt weird to continue to stay home and not contribute much because I couldn't. We are given the ability to work so that we can afford to eat, pay our bills and try to enjoy other things that bring us pleasure. Yet, somehow these days there are people who don't work and can afford more groceries than me. I'm not exactly sure how that's fair. I would love to enjoy more of the fruits of my labor because I work hard. I like the satisfaction of being rewarded for my work and building my life knowing that I accomplished it without a handout.

Working is just an integral part of life. We need people stocking the shelves in grocery stores or fixing our vehicles when they break down. Working stimulates the economy and keeps things moving along. Many companies are hurting today because they are short staffed. Their current employees have to pick up the slack or other companies are forced to change their hours of operation in order to accommodate.

I'm confident that if I wanted to I could fill out an application just about anywhere and get hired because they are in such a desperation for workers. I think it would be a shame for someone who is able to work but would rather live off the government when the job market is so ripe. God is certainly not to blame if you're struggling financially but won't go get a job and work. God has provided an unlimited amount of opportunities for us to hand pick from. I remember a time when I would take any job I could get just because jobs were scarce and I was desperate. Now the tables have turned. The job market is really set up for us to be in control. I would even be willing to bet that your current employer doesn't want to lose you so if you're unhappy you could probably request a few changes or a raise. If you are wanting a different job though, now is probably the best time to play around with different jobs until you find something you like and want to do. What's holding you back? Take back control of your life and show corporate America who the real boss is!

DAY 85

The Struggle Is Real

Matthew 26:41
Watch and pray, that ye enter not into temptation:
the spirit indeed is willing, but the flesh is weak.

he Bible is full of dead ringers! I love how Bible verses can have several different meanings. You can take the same verse and it can have various applications for different seasons of your life. Like today's verse can be interpreted as a warning against temptation. No doubt that would be a great piece of advice to elaborate on, but I really want to focus on the second half of the verse.

Lately I really struggle with my imperfect, selfish, fleshy body that I live in. It has a hard time remembering that it isn't actually in control. It has no problem with letting me know what it wants and makes things practically unbearable until I give in to its demands. It constantly likes to be fed and requires a lot of rest. This is difficult when you want to be productive but the next thing you know you are falling asleep on the couch before your program is over. What about when you make a commitment to help a friend or family member over the weekend and then when the time comes you really want to cancel because you rationalize that you have already worked hard enough during the week. Suddenly you now want to spend your free time relaxing or on a more fun activity. Three days ago when you offered assistance it seemed like a really great idea and you genuinely wanted to help. The spirit is willing but the flesh is weak!

What about when you have a really bad day at work and you want to throw in the towel? Your flesh will get worked up in no time and all rationality flies out the window. The flesh really likes getting those paychecks but it also has a natural proclivity for wanting to be lazy. Deep down you know you need to calm down and stop over reacting but the flesh is so weak. It will literally ruin your life if you let it have complete control.

I have one of the worst cases of sweet tooth imaginable. It feels like my brain is constantly trying to tell me to buy sweets to reward myself. "Hey, you made it through another day, go buy some candy. You deserve it." It's kind of embarrassing how many times that has actually worked! I also have a gym membership. I actually really do enjoy working out because I can relieve some stress and I can feel my body working better. I also have an easier time falling asleep and staying asleep because I am so tired after a workout. I haven't actually gone to the gym in a long time though. I know it's good for me on so many levels and I truly do want to get back into the habit. Once again, the spirit is willing but the flesh is weak! My flesh says," You worked hard enough today." Or "You have things at home you need to do." Now I'm trapped in this cycle of bad habits of giving in to my flesh. It becomes so much harder to regain control of your flesh the longer you let it call the shots!

What about your finances? The flesh loves to be spontaneous and spend money. Then later you regret spending that $50 dollars when you are forced to face your budget. Every little expense adds up so quickly and definitely leaves your pocket way faster than the time it takes to replenish it.

Personally, there are even times when I really want to pray and bear my soul to God but I feel so emotionally drained that it takes a lot of effort to start the conversation. Once again the spirit is willing but the flesh is weak!

I wish I could provide an answer for those of you who know what kind of struggles I'm talking about because you face similar battles. Unfortunately, I don't think there is a magical secret that will solve all your problems or mine. I can only tell you a tiny bit about what helps inspire me to keep trying even when I feel like I'm being defeated. Whenever I feel like my life is spiraling out of control I like to read one of my favorite books called The Slight Edge, by Jeff Olson. It reminds me the importance of taking simple, daily actions that compounded over time will create the results I want. It can work for me or against me and every day I choose which way it will go. I could buy a snack at the gas station or I could resist the urge because I know I set financial and health goals that I'm trying to reach. I could come home from work and plop down on the couch to watch tv or I could find something productive to do that will keep the number of chores from piling up and taking over my weekend. If I choose to talk to God every day even just for a little bit, it is easier than not speaking to Him for several days or longer and then trying to mend things.

Anyway, I highly recommend the book because you can be inspired like I have been to literally start in any area of your life that you want to improve and see that it can be done by starting with small steps. If it took giant leaps and bounds to improve we would give up even quicker because of the effort it would take. Or we might be too intimidated to even begin trying. The Slight Edge also points out that our simple, daily disciplines are easy to do and just as easy not to do which is why the majority doesn't do them. You can beat the majority when it comes to success just by deciding to do what is easy to do and then doing them consistently because that's how the compounding effect comes into play to produce the results you want! So where are you going to be a week from now or a month or a year from now? Are you going to start taking those small, insignificant actions and watch time work for you to get you where you want? Or will you be exactly right where you are now and wishing you had started because you still don't see your goals being accomplished?

Day 86

Saul, Saul, Why Persecutest Thou Me?

Acts 9:1-4

*I*n this passage you read a small excerpt about Saul. He was a known persecutor of Christians. He hunted them down and had them killed. That doesn't seem to be like a very good time to be a Christian in those days! Saul had so much hate in his heart toward God and the children of God to have committed these murders. I remember the first time I learned about Saul. I thought he was going to get it and that God was really going to go after this guy. If anyone deserved the wrath of God, it would be Saul! However, as I kept reading, I was not prepared for the biggest plot twist of all time. By the end of the chapter, God reveals Himself to Saul and Saul converts to Christianity! Then Saul becomes a disciple, changes his name to Paul and helps spread the gospel! Talk about being mind blown! I really didn't know what to make of it all. I was surprised that God would go to such drastic lengths to convert Saul and I thought God could've chosen someone else to convert. Surely, He could've used someone at least whose goals were not to hunt down and murder Christians? People knew who this guy was and that he was bad news!

The crazy part is that I'm really not so different from Saul. I never murdered anyone but I didn't understand Christians until I was converted. I definitely made fun of Christians and I wanted absolutely nothing to do with God. I blamed God for a lot of hurt that I experienced and so little by little I began to decide that I actually didn't believe in God anymore. I thought Christians were crazy to worship someone who didn't exist. I thought church was a scam to collect money and that the congregation was all a fake. I honestly believed that somehow all these people were being tricked too and that they weren't smart enough to realize it. So in a way I persecuted God and other Christians. Unlike Saul, I wasn't well known or very popular. The fact that God sought out Saul and also sought me out is equally surprising. I liked to think I was invisible in school and in life in general. I didn't have very many friends so I was used to being overlooked. Looking back, it would have made more sense for God to have treated me just like everyone else did. Plot twist! I wasn't invisible to God all along. He picked lots of different people from the Bible to serve Him from all kinds of different backgrounds. God even picked small, insignificant people that nobody ever thought twice about. People who were just like me. Now that I know God a little better, it isn't so surprising after all that He sought me out. Not because I think I'm any better than anyone else, but because that's just God doing what He does best. He loves like no one else can and He extends a hand to everyone even though not everyone will take His hand and decide to follow Him.

Saul (Paul) had a lot of challenges to overcome once he was converted. People didn't trust him. They wanted to kill him once he was captured because of his hateful behavior towards Christians. I imagine it took a long time for him to redeem himself in the eyes of the public. I don't blame them at all for being skeptical and cautious! Sometimes I think I am still guilty and persecute God, unintentionally but unfortunately. Every time that I hesitate to speak up about my beliefs is a persecution. Not that I'm ashamed, but the subject of religion in general is a very touchy subject. I may not be killed for my beliefs like in Paul's day, but if I'm not careful I could end up facing serious repercussions depending on the situation. Every time that I delay acting on what I feel God is leading me to do is a type of persecution. I'm acting as if serving Him is less important than other things that I allow to steal my attention.

Maybe you can relate. I'm not perfect and neither are you. You could substitute your name instead of Saul's in the verse, "Saul, Saul, why persecutest thou me?" If you're being honest with yourself and God, you could probably think of at least one circumstance where you are guilty of persecuting God too. Since we can't change the past we must focus on the future. Thankfully, the future is full of lots of opportunities to do better! The best part of it all is that if God was willing to forgive Saul and dramatically change the trajectory of his life, then He is more than willing to do the same for us. There is no act so heinous that we could commit that would put us beyond redemption. God is God and He is greater than any sin. He loves doing the seemingly impossible and throwing a plot twist in the stories of our lives. In what ways have you persecuted God? What plot twists has God surprised you with in your life? Do you see how God has sought after you and helped prepare you for an entirely different life than the one you were living before He got your attention?

Directionally Challenged

Psalm 23:3
He restoreth my soul:
he leadeth me in the paths of righteousness for his name's sake.

I really like this passage because I really love all of Psalm 23. Is there possibly someone reading this that needs their soul restored? I know I sure do lately. Life and unfavorable circumstances just have a way of beating us up and discouraging us. They can definitely make things difficult for a while. It's totally normal to be discouraged and have your focus on your problems. We're all human and not perfect, right? The problem with problems is that they take our focus off of God. When we're worried about finances, relationship issues, sickness, etc our mental energy becomes drained and it's hard to think about how God is going to take care of us. Deep down, we know He will never leave us or forsake us, so why would our current situations be any different?

I don't know much about navigation. In fact I'm really good at getting lost. I have to fully rely on a GPS whenever I travel somewhere new. Even then I still get a little lost. Especially when I'm really close to my destination! It can be so frustrating but it makes for some good laughs afterwards. I really don't know how I manage it. Sometimes its construction that confuses me or some other car won't let me over to get to my exit in time because I lost track of time and didn't realize I was coming up on it. A lot of times I have gotten lost because of my GPS! At times it makes me go way out of my way instead of the most direct route while other times it tries to take me down a road that isn't a road at all! With how directionally challenged I am I really have no desire to test out my lack of skills in the wilderness. I have a lot of respect for people who could get dropped off in the middle of the woods and find their way back out because I wouldn't be able to do it! I'd like to think that maybe I could survive with a compass but that's just wishful thinking!

What about how years ago when ships sailed the vast oceans and had to rely on the starts at night or the placement of the sun during the day? I'm pretty sure I would just die at sea! The point is even the most experienced sailor would wind up lost if they didn't follow "the North Star." An accomplished explorer could struggle to find his bearings without any sense of direction or even a compass. I would definitely never reach any of my destinations without a GPS! The reason is because they would be taking their eyes and focus off of their guides. God is like our own North Star. As long as we continue looking up at Him for guidance for our lives we can't get lost. With Him pointing us in the right direction just like a compass, we will never go wrong. God is even better than a mostly reliable GPS because God will ensure that we reach every destination flawlessly.

I have had my fair share of financial struggles but even in the midst of them I could take some of my focus off of worrying about how I'm going to fix it when I remember that God has always met all my needs. I continue to expect Him to come through by providing in new ways that I could never predict or solve on my own! When I sometimes get bummed about my diabetes, the situation doesn't seem too bad when I think of how others have way worse conditions that they're facing. On most days I choose to remind myself that God has a bigger plan even though I don't see it or understand it yet. I never want to belittle anyone or their circumstances. I just want to encourage others to take their worries to God and lay them at His feet. When you take the burdens off yourself by looking past your own problems and fix your eyes back on God, it's kinda hard to stay discouraged for very long. I know this to be true because He has helped me countless times. He has restored my soul every time when I get drained. He gives me a peace of mind and peace in my soul. That's how I know I will get to the other side of each struggle I face.

I never really gave much thought to the last part of the verse before. God is promising to see us through our battles and He is promising to restore us because His name is at stake. "For His name's sake," means that if He were to abandon us now when we need Him the most, then we could actually doubt Him. We could question His love for us or honestly any of His other promises He has made throughout the Bible. Since He was so serious about this promise that He was willing to stake His name or essentially all of His credibility on it then that means that God being who He is, He will always fulfill His promises. There's literally no way possible that God will ever turn back on His word!

A majority of the time I would get lost using my GPS is when I was really close to my destination. As frustrating as it would be to be so close and get lost, I knew it would make no sense to give up now. I always pushed through and stuck with it until I finally got there. This is where a lot of us are spiritually. We are so close to our destination (gaining the victory over our struggles) that it doesn't make sense to give up now. Especially not now that we know God will get us there!

A Woman After God's Own Heart

Acts 13:22
And when he had removed him, he raised up unto them
David to be their king; to whom also he gave testimony,
and said, I have found David the son of Jesse,
a man after mine own heart, which shall fulfill all my will.

The life of David has always intrigued me and inspired me in many ways. God used him to do incredible things. One of the most memorable would probably be when he slayed Goliath. He was still just a kid then! When he grew up he eventually became a king and it was through his lineage that God decided His son Jesus, the savior of the world would be born! On the other hand, David's life was far from free of his own share of trials and tribulations. I'm so thankful the Bible includes accounts of many people who were not perfect or entirely faithful to God. These people, including David, made plenty of bad decisions for one reason or another. That makes them so much more relatable. Also, it's comforting to know that no matter how bad you mess things up, God is still willing to forgive you and use you to do great things!

I can't think of a higher compliment than for David to have been called a man after God's own heart, which is why for several years, one of my deepest ambitions has been to be a woman after God's own heart. I've never been exactly sure what it means or how to fall into that category, but I'm learning more every day. I think a large portion of that involves learning how to love yourself and accept yourself even during the times you are most unlovable because God created you and loves you. How can you expect to grow closer to God when you are at war with yourself, knowing that God doesn't make mistakes? Therefore, just because you make mistakes, that doesn't make you a mistake.

In addition, to be after God's heart, I think you have to desire His companionship. There have been several instances where I turned my back on God. Each time, even though I had strayed so far from Him, I would miss the closeness I once shared with Him. Unfortunately for me, I'm really stubborn and I would go long periods of time without communicating with God even when I desperately wanted to. I don't know if shame, fear, pride, or disappointment kept me at bay, but whatever the reason, I remember all too well the tugging on my heart telling me to go back to Him and mend things. Thankfully, eventually, I do because God finds a way to show me that He loves me and it's so hard to keep pushing someone away who refuses to stop loving you or ever give up on you.

To be after God's heart, I think another factor is that you need to be willing to chase God. A lot of times we probably take God for granted because we know He will always be there for us so we only go to Him when we're ready. We wait until we've exhausted ourselves completely when really we need to chase down God during the good times and the bad times. When I think of the phrase, "to be after," I picture someone running towards something out of desire or necessity with a sense of urgency. I'm not saying I believe God would ever run away from us, but I want to stress the importance with which we need to practice creating the habit of running to God. It's easy to praise God during the good times and just as easy to be distant with God during difficult times. Even when you're sort of standing on middle ground when nothing is actually bad in your life, yet nothing new and exciting is happening either, that is just as important of a time to seek out God. He wants us to cast all our cares upon Him. Not just the good or bad, but also the blah. You know, when things just feel weird.

When we chase after God we need to bear in mind that He is the answer to all our worries or needs. That is why we need a sense of urgency because we need Him. The missing link though, is desire. You can chase God all you want and not find Him if the desire isn't there. You can go to church, read your Bible, tithe, listen to worship music and pray all you want to because you k now those are the right things to do. Just going through the motions won't get you to God's heart. He never intended for us to serve Him out of obligation. He wants us to serve Him willingly out of the desires of our hearts. In other words because we choose to.

In another sense, "to be after" something implies that an object is hidden, lost or well protected. When an object is lost it is imperative that it be found. Not too long ago I lost my truck keys which were already my backup set! I searched inside and outside my house with increasing intensity several times over. I didn't just want to find my keys, I needed to find my keys. Not only did I have an appointment that morning, but how else would I be able to reach any other destination I needed to go to in the near future? I was so tempted to give up out of anger at myself for my own carelessness and frustration. Oddly enough, I was driven with increasing intensity to find them the longer I spent looking for them just as badly as I was tempted to lose all hope and give up. That is how we need to seek God's heart. Just as I was almost convinced I would never find my keys, I finally found them after raking through a pile of leaves. I'm still convinced I only found them because I didn't give up. We need to approach God's heart with the same mindset. Never give up! Keep going! Don't lose hope! Refuse to stop even when things look dim. In the end you will find Him! You will find God's heart! You will get your prayers answered! God even says those that seek Him will find Him. Seeking is the act of looking not the act of giving up!

How would you describe your spiritual life right now? Have you been after God's heart or have you given up? I believe David found

God's heart! He lived an incredibly blessed life. Can you look back on your life and say you have been incredibly blessed? Sure, you can but can you also see where there are areas that can be improved? I think we can always improve because we will never reach perfection as long as we are here on this earth.

DAY 89

Are You Sharp or Are You Dull?

Proverbs 27:17
Iron sharpeneth iron;
so a man sharpeneth the countenance of his friend.

You have probably heard the saying, "Birds of a feather flock together." Or "You are who you associate with." I can't stress how true these sayings are. You will adopt the habits of the people you spend the most time with. You could even adopt the same thought processes and live a lifestyle similar to those of your friends. This could be a good thing or it could be a bad thing. If your friends encourage you, support your dreams and goals, and can give you great advice, then keep those people in your life!

I would even take it a few steps further and suggest that you even make friends with people who live lives similar to the life you want. You will meet people at all different stages of life. Maybe you are not married or don't have any kids yet. Make friends with people who are married with children. That way you can learn from their example. You will get a glimpse of how your future could look. Also, you will get to decide if you want to adopt some of their habits or pick what you would change when your time comes. This is just one example. I believe this concept can be applicable in any area of your life. If you want to be healthier, adopt friends who like to be active. If you find yourself being down and feeling gloomy, find some new people to associate with who are usually positive and uplifting. If you find yourself struggling financially, seek out someone you might know who doesn't seem to be struggling as much. You never know, they might have some good advice on how to handle money or some other way to help you that you never thought of before.

Friends are supposed to have your back during the hard times, not just when it's fun. They are supposed to add value to your life and help you become the best possible version of yourself that you can be. I'm fortunate enough to have a handful of friends like this. In a lot of instances they have never given up on me even when I have given up on myself. To them, it doesn't matter if we haven't spoken recently or regularly, but if I needed someone to talk to they were still there for me. Sometimes I'm not too sure if I add any value to their lives, but I try to do so. I believe friendships are like any other relationship. You can't just be the one to take all the time or be in it for how it benefits you. You need to give as well. That's the whole point of Proverbs 27:17. Just like iron sharpens iron, we are meant to sharpen our friends. If you're putting in all the work, eventually, you will get dull. If you have friends that never reach out to check on you but expect you to always reach out, you will get emotionally drained.

I'm naturally more of an introvert. I can have more fun sitting at home in my pj's reading a book than if I were to be out in the public doing things and surrounded by people. I'm more at ease being alone because it feels more peaceful. I still have to be careful because I can still get dull. I might not be giving anything but I'm also not receiving either. If I'm not socializing with positive influences, then I'm missing opportunities to be challenged to reach new heights. The opposite is true too. When I isolate too often, I'm not influencing anyone else for the better.

I do believe some alone time is healthy. That's how I recharge. I can be lazy and rest or catch up on cleaning the house. Also, when I'm home, I know that I'm not spending money which is great because I'm trying to hit some financial goals! However, I fully recognize that I wouldn't be a fraction of the person I am today if it wasn't for the influence of my friends. If it wasn't for us sharpening each other throughout the years I don't know who I would be. I know I wouldn't have the courage to chase my dreams and without my belief in obtaining those dreams, I would be a very empty, miserable person.

At the end of the day, I hope my friends can say that I added value to their lives too. Where do you currently stand? Are you sharp? Are you on top of your game or have you allowed some influence of the wrong people to wear on you and make you dull? Are there some people in your life that you need to spend less time with and others that you should spend more time with?

It's Ok To Fall Apart

2 Timothy 1:7
*For God hath not given us the spirit of fear;
but of power, and of love, and of a sound mind.*

It's ok to fall apart sometimes. Tacos do and we still love them!

(Credit: Facebook)

This devotional is unlike anything I've ever written before. Nor is it one that I really would have imagined myself writing about. However, it is about some things that I've been experiencing and making progress toward overcoming so I hope that what I'm learning could possibly help somebody else. This would be the subject of mental health. I am aware of the fact that it is real and it is important. I hope to continue understanding it because there was a time not long ago that I did not understand it.

For several years I watched it take a toll on my grandmother. Words can't really describe how it feels to watch someone you love with your entire heart become an entirely different person than who you were used to. I truly believe I did my best to love her anyway and not treat her any differently. She was still here and deserved love and affection even if she didn't act or think like she used to. My family always tried to get her the care she needed and I lived for those little glimpses of her "old self" that would occasionally shine through. Even though she was giving up on herself I never gave up on her. I believed she was still there and she would come back to us. Honestly, I couldn't understand what she was going through and how difficult it must have been for her. Looking back, from what I know about my grandmother, I do believe it is entirely possible that she burned herself out and didn't take care of herself for too long. She was incredibly amazing in every way. She did a lot of things for a lot of people. She always treated people kindly and could light up a room. She had the best laugh and was so animated when telling a story. I could go on forever about her. I wish she could've seen herself the way I still saw her. The last few years she was with us she would barely leave the house. She became more and more dependent upon my grandpa. She was still capable of doing many things if she wanted to she just wouldn't. In some ways I was losing her before she even went to live in Heaven and I tried to enjoy whatever time I was able to have with her. I miss her every single day.

Lately, what I've been learning is that poor mental health is just another ailment in this fallen, imperfect world. Just like cancer is real and those individuals need treatment, your brain can definitely be affected and become sick. It could be genetic or it could be caused due to trauma. Whatever the cause it is important to take care of yourself and get the help you need. The reason I say this is because I'm learning how to do it too. For a while now, I have been in denial about my condition. You can bet I have probably tried every trick in the book to delay getting to the point I'm currently at. All I managed to do was cause things to get worse for myself. I'm way too stubborn so maybe I needed to hit rock bottom and fall apart so that I would be forced to get myself help. I realized not only did I need to do it for myself but also for my family. They didn't deserve the person they were getting. I was always tired and moody. They deserved the old me who was more patient and understanding.

I knew all too well that my focus and ability to do my job efficiently was slipping as well. I didn't think I could miss time from work to take care of myself but after watching a coworker do it, I realized that it just might be totally possible for me too. I'm still not sure that I acted on courage to seek help but I am glad I did. I still feel weak but I am getting stronger every day. I am optimistic about the future again and I believe I can and will get my life back on track.

I have a close friend I have been confiding in and she has helped make a huge impact in my life lately. She has never judged me because she has experienced some of the same things. She has helped pave the way for me to follow and made the journey a little less scary by allowing me to see some things from a different perspective. So, yes, I'm taking medication and I'm seeing a therapist that I really like. This therapist believes I'm not a lost cause and her confidence helps me to actually be excited about our future sessions so that I can finally have some victory and make progress. So, whatever your mind is telling you it isn't true. You are not going crazy. You can get help. You are not too messed up. It is ok to take medication. It is ok to get therapy. You are worth it and things can get better!

Today, I have reminded myself once again that I'm never going to be perfect and it really is ok. So my next goal is to stop trying so hard to be perfect but to still keep trying. By that I mean still forgiving myself and others. Still putting one foot in front of the other even if it is small steps. If the only thing extra you accomplish is washing some dishes, then be proud of yourself for doing it. I had to slow my life down for a little bit and I only did what I felt like I could do and I was ok if I didn't do everything that needed to be done. I'm glad for what I did do. It felt good and those were steps in the right direction. You have to start focusing on how far you have come and not at how far you still have to go because there used to be a time when you wanted to be where you are right now! Be proud of where you are right now!